Canning and Preserving
without Sugar

by Norma M. MacRae, R.D.

Updated to meet latest U.S.D.A.
canning recommendations

Pacific Search Press

Pacific Search Press, 222 Dexter Avenue North,
    Seattle, Washington 98109
© 1982 by Norma M. MacRae
Printed in the United States of America

Second printing 1983

Designed by Judy Petry

Library of Congress Cataloging in Publication Data

MacRae, Norma M., 1924—
    Canning and preserving without sugar.

    Bibliography: p.
    Includes index.
    1. Canning and preserving. 2. Sugar-free
diet—Recipes. I. Title
TX603.M23 1982   641.4'2   82-12433
ISBN 0-914718-71-1

Contents

15   914

Preface

This book is for everyone who wants to avoid sugar—people who are aware of how much sugar they've been eating, how harmful it can be, and who want to cut down—diabetics, hypoglycemics, natural food enthusiasts, and anyone concerned about good nutrition, good taste, and good health.

Traditional canning methods call for large amounts of sugar. Juice-canned fruits and jams made with honey are available commercially, but often they cost so much that many people are reluctant to buy them and many others refuse. A cookbook was needed that would show how to preserve fruit easily at home, without sugar, for a reasonable price. This book was written to answer that need.

These recipes took many hours to test and involved a fair number of failures. Fruit-juice sweetened recipes were not easy to develop, and it was difficult to create mixtures using honey without overpowering the natural flavor of the fruit. Here, then, is a collection of good-tasting, reliable recipes for canned fruits, jellies, jams, pickles, and relishes the whole family will enjoy. Best of all, they are made without adding table sugar (or, in many cases, salt).

Before You Begin

What to Use for Sweetening

Liquid must be added when canning fruit. Early diabetic fruit was packed in water, but the fruit tasted just like it sounds—watery! To process fruit this way, be sure it is eating-ripe, and pack it into jars in slices, or other small pieces, so little liquid is needed. This gives almost a juice pack, but, without any added sweetening, will not enhance the fruit flavor.

Several liquids can be used to make syrup, including natural fruit juice, concentrated fruit juice, honey-sweetened water, and actual fruit such as thin applesauce. To make the most of the natural sweetening in ripe fruit, pack it in small slices or pieces to allow more of the fruit's sugar to go into the liquid, and more of the liquid's sweetening into the fruit. The result is most tasty!

When selecting fruit juice, use natural juice, if available—apple juice with canned apples, for example. This will give the most natural fruit flavor; adding a small amount of lemon juice will enhance the flavor even more. Try small batches using various juices. What sounds good doesn't always taste as good; you may find that adding a spice helps perk up the flavor. Whole cloves, grated fresh ginger root, or whole cinnamon sticks can work wonders. Although the Washington State Extension Service does not recommend it, I like to add a *few* pits to canned fruit to create a pleasant, almond-like taste. You can also add peach or apricot pits to other fruit for taste variety.

Frozen Juice

Concentrated apple juice, orange juice, and pineapple juice are all available in the freezer of your grocery store and should be used as soon as possible after thawing for best flavor. Most frozen juices are meant to be diluted with three volumes of water. Used undiluted or partly diluted, they make a concentrated sweetener for canning or preserving. Just be sure they are labeled "pure juice."

Fruit Essence

Some health food stores sell canned fruit essences. These are much like frozen concentrated juices, although they may be even more concentrated. Check the dilution suggested to see how they compare with those in the grocery store (check the price, too). In most cases, frozen concentrated juices have a more natural flavor than canned essences. Taste these before using. If you do use them, dilute to the same strength as frozen concentrates (four times fresh strength) and follow recipes as given.

Canned Juice

Many bottled and canned juices are not pure. Read the label carefully to be sure you are getting pure juice with no sugar added. A number of juice combinations are now appearing on the market. Apple-pear would be an excellent choice for canning pears, and pineapple-grapefruit a possible choice for freezing grapefruit and/or fresh pineapple. Keep watching to see what new mixtures are introduced that might be good to use.

Date Sugar

Date sugar can be added to sweeten jam and preserves. This is a pure, natural product made by drying and grinding dates. It has a distinctive, slightly acid taste and must be used with lemon juice added to help mask this flavor.

Other Dried Fruits for Sweetening

Commercially dried fruits (available in the grocery store) are treated with sulphur dioxide to prevent darkening. Untreated dried fruits will be much darker and probably a bit lower in moisture (some may be a lot lower). If you plan to use home-dried fruit for preserves or cooking, allow extra moisture in the recipe unless it is one that you want to simmer down for reduced volume. Allow at least one tablespoon extra liquid per cup of dried fruit. The color of the finished food will be more intense (darker) with home-dried or unsulphured dried fruits, but this substitution should not affect the taste.

Honey Syrup

Any fruit can be canned with honey syrup; there need be no change in directions given for both hot pack and cold or raw pack when it is used. I have not emphasized its use because those who do not want to use refined sugar may not want to (or cannot, in the case of the diabetic or hypoglycemic) use honey either. (While a naturally occurring sugar, honey still adds highly concentrated sweetening to the natural sweetness of fruit.)

Fruits canned with medium strength honey syrup are very good if enough lemon juice is added to disguise the taste of the honey. With honey, the sugar content will be greater than with juice pack (and the calories greater), the color won't be as apt to fade (as it will using juice), and it will taste more satisfying to the sugar user than the less sweet fruit-juice pack.

Special Ingredients

Lemon Juice and Dried Citrus Rind

Many of these recipes call for lemon juice. Frozen lemon juice can be used with complete satisfaction; ideally, however, use fresh juice and strain it to remove seeds and pulp. Grate the rind before squeezing the lemon and dehydrate or freeze the grated rind for later use. Commercial orange and lemon peel products all contain sugar, but it is very simple to dry your own. Follow the instructions given below and store in a closed container in a cool, dark place. (I have kept home-dried rind for over two years and found it just as good as when first prepared.)

Dried Citrus Rind

Lemons, oranges, grapefruit (or mixed citrus fruit)   1 or more

Using fine grater, grate rind onto nonstick cookie sheet, spreading over sheet to give even grating without lumps. Place sheet on top rack of oven preheated to 200°. Turn down to 150° when you put in rind, and leave to dry for 1½ to 2 hours until rind feels dry–and not sticky. Remove from oven, allow to cool. Break up lumps with the bottom of a glass tumbler. Place dried rind in tightly-covered jar and store in cool, dark place.
Note: Color will fade if left where rind gets light. A brown bottle will help prevent this. Rind will dry to about half the volume of fresh. *Use half the amount of fresh lemon rind called for in a recipe,* slightly more than half the amount of orange rind and slightly less than half the amount of grapefruit rind (stronger flavor). Or let dried rind soak in warm water for 20 to 30 minutes and use as fresh.

Food Coloring

A few of these recipes suggest adding vegetable food coloring. Colors sold in grocery stores are artificial colors, not from vegetable sources. If you don't want to use anything that is manufactured like this, a totally natural color can be obtained with the use of items found in most kitchens (see suggestions below).

Red: Rhubarb and berries tend to fade when cooked without sugar. To restore the color naturally, take beet liquid and simmer it down to half the original volume. Add the concentrated beet liquid to the mixtures you wish to color (one tablespoon liquid will color one cup or more), but be sure to add spices or extra lemon juice to help disguise any flavor carried over from the beets.

Yellow: A number of spices will give yellow color, including saffron, mustard, turmeric, and cumin. Since saffron is so costly, mustard and turmeric have strong flavors which are hard to disguise, and cumin also has a flavor which some people notice, none of these is ideal. If you can afford it, saffron is most useful, and a minute amount will give concentrated color. Cumin is probably the next best choice, unless you have a strong ingredient such as vinegar to help disguise the mustard or turmeric taste.

Green: Peelings of zucchini squash have an intense green color. These can be cooked until soft and pureed for use as a coloring agent. Again, you may have to adjust the recipe with lemon juice or additional herbs to cover any taste which the peel may have added.

Salt and Salt Substitutes

Table salt (sodium chloride) is usually processed to add iodine for prevention of goiter. It does not make a good pickle; get noniodized or pickling salt—a coarse salt ideal for pickles. This is for sale in most large groceries during canning season.

Sea salt contains chemicals other than sodium chloride, and is not a good choice for pickling. Kosher salt will work, though. A salt substitute can be used in any of these recipes, provided it is acceptable to your taste. I have found only one I think good enough. It can be obtained by mail order from Johnny's Enterprises, Inc., 319 E. 25th St., Tacoma, Washington 98421. It is called "Healthline Salt Replacement" and contains potassium, but does not have the bitter aftertaste of most salt substitutes. I have used it in pickles and sauces with success. Use this salt substitute as you would use salt called for in the recipes. The sodium values of each recipe are given at the bottom, provided that no real salt is added.

Vinegar

There are three basic vinegars on the market. Most people buy and use cider vinegar (made from apples) or wine vinegar (made from red or white wine). For pickling and meat sauces use distilled vinegar (sometimes called pickling vinegar), which is a little milder and will not discolor the food being cooked or pickled. Distilled vinegar does not have the sharp bite of cider and wine vinegars, partly because it is lower in acetic acid (4 percent compared to 5 or 6 percent).

You can easily make herb vinegar by adding not more than two teaspoons herb per cup vinegar (cider or wine) and allowing it to stand for up to a month or until the flavor suits you. Do not use this herb vinegar in pickle or sauce recipes, as its strength is uncertain and results will be, too.

Gelatin or Agar-Agar

Gelatin is used in many sugarless jams (and other naturally sweetened products) to help keep the liquid from separating from the solids, thus giving a watery consistency. If you want to avoid animal products (gelatin is made from animals), use agar-agar instead. The easiest form to use is Chinese agar-agar which comes in sticks (usually two in a package) and can be purchased in health food stores or Oriental food stores. One-half stick can be dissolved in one-half cup of liquid and that liquid must then be accounted for in your recipe. It may be difficult to dissolve, however. Break it into small pieces—using scissors helps. Place them in a small bowl and add liquid (you could use some of the fruit juice called for in the recipe); allow it to stand for at least thirty minutes. Then stir and slowly heat to complete dissolving the agar. This will replace one tablespoon gelatin (one envelope) in a recipe and will give an even firmer jell at warmer temperatures.

Spices

Pure spices are not supposed to contain additives of any kind. On the other hand, spice mixtures (herb mixes, for example) may contain both salt and sugar in some form. Be sure you buy pure spice and keep it in a dark, cool place in a tightly covered container. Spices are aromatic and will lose their flavor over a period of time. Exposure to light and heat speeds up this process, as well as causing color changes in some things (my dried parsley turned white after being left for several months where the sun occasionally shone on the jar). Of course, the taste will still be there, but with the color gone, it loses some appeal.

Don't buy cheap spices. Stick with brand names for top quality, and avoid products on sale, as they may be old and less potent. Buying good spices is an investment and if you care for them as suggested, they will add enjoyment to your food for several years.

How to Choose Fruits for Canning and Preserving

If this is your first home-canning season, you may be wondering how to find the best varieties of fruit. Of course, the first concern is flavor. Fruit should be eating-ripe. Tree-ripened fruit is sweetest and should be first choice. It shouldn't be bruised or overripe (although you can use slightly overripe fruit for part of a jam recipe, overripe fruit won't always give good results).

Eat a piece of fruit from the source you are considering. It should taste delicious! This can't be done until the canning season, but do some reading and asking questions beforehand so you'll know what variety you want to use. One of the best places to learn about local varieties and their availability is the Public Library. It will have bulletins put out by your state and federal governments giving information on various regional food crops. The next best places to start looking are nursery catalogs, local nurseries who know what grows best in your area, and area farmers. Get acquainted with local people and find out what fruits they use for canning and jam. You might even want to ask your district's Agricultural Extension Agent or your community college about classes offered.

If you have a neighbor or friend who offers to give you fruit (or perhaps you have your own), use it—but you may have to change your idea of what to make with it after trying some. Certain apples, for instance, are good for eating, cooking, and freezing; others are good only for eating. Try small batches (see Index for Trial Batch recipes) to see what can best be done with what you have—far better than making a large batch and finding out you don't like the results.

If you plan to buy fruit to process, sort out and use the ripest first, allowing the rest to ripen before cooking. Work in small batches as the fruit ripens. Use pint or half-pint jars, unless you have a very large family, and be sure to use any juice or syrup along with the fruit, as between one-fourth and one-half the water-soluble vitamins and other nutrients are found there.

Fruit processed this way won't taste as sweet as that canned with sugar. It is possible to can, preserve, even make pickles, with fruit juices and honey, but the sweetening you'll add still amounts to much less than sugar-canned fruits contain. For this reason, people who use lots of sugar may not think your home-canned fruit, jams, jellies, and pickles are sweet enough. Others, with more finely tuned tastes, will applaud!

The following pages offer details to help you decide which fruits to choose. But remember, your area may offer even better choices located with help from your nurseryman, library, or neighbor.

Apples

Early Crop: Available mid-July to early August. Yellow Transparent and Lodi are among these early apples. They are noted for making good green apple pie and applesauce, but are not as good for eating and keep poorly. These can be allowed to ripen and then frozen in slices (with lemon juice to prevent browning), in unbaked pies, or in applesauce (green or ripe).

Middle Crop: Available mid-August through early September. Gravenstein, Jonathan, McIntosh, Rome and Rome Beauty, Yellow Delicious, and Winesap are good for both eating and canning or freezing. They keep well if left in a cool, well ventilated place and can be used in all recipes calling for apples.

Late Crop: Available late September through the end of October. King, Granny Smith, Snow, and Wealthy can be cooked or eaten raw equally well, and can be stored in a cool, well ventilated place for use all winter.

Note: Red Delicious apples are not included in this list, as they don't cook or can well, although raw they make very good eating. Yellow (Golden) Delicious apples are not the same fruit as Red Delicious and they *are* good cooking and canning apples, although they lack the stronger apple flavor found in Gravenstein, Jonathan, Rome, or Winesap varieties, which are preferable for that reason. To test for ripeness, take a bite. If it doesn't taste delicious, it isn't ripe. Look for color and firmness. If you press the fruit and it doesn't give (feel slightly soft), it will not be a good choice. The background of the apple should show some yellow, too. Fruit picked green will never develop the same flavor as that allowed to fully ripen on the tree.

Table 1 can help you decide which apples to buy.

Apricots

Moorpack, Perfection, and Tilton are the best apricot varieties available in northwest markets. The Tilton is usually smaller and will pack more into a jar than larger types, but for flavor all are good. A few pits left in the jar when canning apricots help give more flavor than when the fruit is canned alone. At their peak in July, apricots must be completely yellow, but not too soft or they are overripe. On the other hand, if apricots are picked too green, they will never reach ideal sweetness. Try to choose fruit which has been allowed to ripen on the tree and has not been held long before you get it. Remember to taste a sample before you buy.

Berries

Strawberries: Look for local berries to see which you prefer. (In our area I like the Marshalls—they are red and sweet all the way through and have no hard core section to be discarded. These are early berries and may be available late June and into early July.) One of the best ways to tell if strawberries are ripe is to smell them. They have a delicious smell with a sweetish tang when ripe. It is a very strong smell—not like that from less ripe berries. They should also be fully red. Partly green berries will not be as sweet, even if they ripen after picking. Berries should be soft but not mushy—then they are overripe. Try to get them directly from the patch; they are so superior to those in grocery stores, you will never be satisfied with anything else again. Strawberries do not keep well when picked fully ripe. Plan to use them within a day or two, or some may mold.

Frozen whole berries are fully ripe when frozen. You can use these for making jams and sauces during the winter with good results.

Raspberries: The red raspberry is best for canning, jam, or jelly. The Cuthbert variety has the most typical flavor. While not as heavy-bearing as some, many people think of it as the ideal raspberry. Cuthbert hybrids may be your best choices. Check with your local nurserymen for what is available and what grows best in your area. Raspberries are very easy to grow, so you might want to consider raising your own. They are satisfactory shrubs for small areas, but do need water and fertilizer in winter. Otherwise, if you can find a "U-pick" patch, you'll save a lot of money. Ripe raspberries are deep in color, firm to touch, and taste sweet. If too dark, they may be overripe and will make poor jam and jelly. Raspberries are available from early to mid-June through July depending on climate.

Loganberries and Other Thornless Berries: Boysenberries, loganberries, Olympic berries, and Young berries are among these thornless types. They are sweet, juicy, and when vine-ripened are excellent choices for canning and preserving. Check to learn which varieties grow well in your area. They are not hard to grow, but do take a bit more space than raspberries and require the same culture. These berries are ripe when they taste sweet and are very juicy. If picked underripe, they will never achieve the same sweetness as when left on the vine to mature. They are available late August and into early September.

Blackberries: Cascade, Olallie, Himalaya, and Thornless Cory are all in the blackberry class. These have smaller seeds than the loganberry group, and therefore make good jam and jelly that tends to be seedy. They do not handle well and may not be available in most stores, but there might be places where you could pick your own (cheaper, too). These bushes will also do well in your own garden and take culture similar to raspberries. Blackberries should be picked totally ripe and used at once. If they are not completely black and soft, they are not fully ripe. To get the sweetest taste, let them stay on the vine until they are so juicy that when you pick them, your fingers get stained with juice. These are later berries, available into September in most areas.

Blueberries (and Huckleberries):   There are several varieties of domesticated (hybrid) blueberries and size varies greatly from one to another. Don't let the size of the berry influence you too much—some of the

Table 1
A Guide to Apple Varieties

Variety	Main Season	Flavor & Texture
Cortland	Oct.-Jan.	Mild, tender
Red Delicious	Sept.-June	Sweet, mellow
Golden Delicious	Sept.-May	Sweet, semifirm
Granny Smith	Apr.-July	Tart, crisp
Gravenstein	July-Sept.	Tart, crisp
Jersey Red	Oct.-Apr.	Mild, firm
Jonathan	Sept.-Jan.	Tart, tender
McIntosh	Sept.-June	Slightly tart, tender
Newtown Pippin	Sept.-June	Slightly tart, firm
Rome Beauty	Oct.-June	Slightly tart, firm
Stayman	Oct.-Mar.	Tart, semifirm
Winesap	Oct.-June	Slightly tart, firm
Yellow Transparent	July-Aug.	Tart, soft
York Imperial	Oct.-Apr.	Tart, firm

Source: Kyle D. Fulwiler. *The Apple Cookbook*, Seattle: Pacific Search Press, 1980.

Raw	Baking	Sauce	Freezing
Excel.	Good	V. good	V. good
Excel.	Poor	Fair	Fair
Excel.	V. good	V. good	V. good
V. good	V. good	V. good	V. good
Good	Good	Good	Good
Good	Excel.	V. good	V. good
V. good	Poor	V. good	V. good
Excel.	Fair	Good	Good
V. good	V. good	Excel.	Excel.
Good	Excel.	V. good	V. good
V. good	Good	Good	Good
Excel.	Good	Good	V. good
Poor	Poor	Good	Poor
Fair	Good	V. good	Good

largest, most beautiful blueberries have less flavor than smaller ones. Blueberries must be completely ripe before picking—this means no red left and the blue is very dark. They will be fairly soft. If in doubt, eat one to see if they taste sweet; if they don't, quit picking (or don't buy them). Wild blueberries and huckleberries have more definite flavor, may be sweeter, but are usually seedier than hybrids. Blueberries are generally available late July through August. Check with local farmers or a nurseryman to see when peak ripening occurs in your area. Huckleberries may not ripen until late August, depending on climate.

Cherries

Cherries should be dead-ripe before they are picked. They must be juicy and sweet, yet still fairly firm. If they are very soft, they are overripe. Dark varieties should be very dark before they are picked. If they show bright red, they are underripe. Cherries come in three colors and have different ripening times. The sour, red, pie cherries are usually an early crop (June to mid-July), but without sugar it is difficult to get these sweet enough unless you add honey. Don't try canning these in juice-syrup. Pale Royal Anne cherries have a delicious, mild flavor and are excellent canned alone or used with other fruits such as fruit cocktail. Bing and Lambert are dark red, sweet cherries that make good eating and are readily available. While Royal Anne cherries are on the market in July, most Bings and Lamberts are just appearing in late July and into August. These large, dark fruits are excellent processed in any way: canned, frozen whole (see section on freezing), made into jam or preserves, or added to other fruits in fruit cocktail. Incidentally, these will color pale fruits. You might freeze a few for later use in fruit cocktail; they will give a very attractive pale pink color to the fruit syrup.

Grapes

Table grapes are available in green and red as well as purple (blue-black), and come seedless and seeded. Ninety percent of the world's grape crop consists of one type: the European grape, now also called the California grape. What you want for eating fresh and what you want for canning may differ. For canning, choose seedless. These include Perlette (green-white, available late May through June), Black Beauty (purple, small, available May and early June), and Thompson (light green, small, available June to October). There are two new, red, seedless varieties: Flame (mid-June through August) and Ruby (mid-August to January). If you are going to cook grapes for juice, seeded varieties are fine. Concord grape varieties include Exotic and Ribier, the first available in summer from June through August, and the second a winter grape, available July through February. Don't rely on color alone when choosing grapes. When the color seems right, taste one from the end of the bunch—if it is sweet, the grapes are ripe.

Nectarines

These newer fruits are in our markets in canning lots, but there is usually not much choice in varieties. You must be sure they are sweet and ripe—bite into one before you buy a batch. Many that look and smell good don't taste as good. They should be soft when pressed and should smell sweet. Also, there should be no green around the stem. (Perhaps there are surer tests for ripeness, but I haven't been able to discover them.) Nectarines are available in early August in most areas.

Peaches

Peaches come in two types: freestone (the fruit comes away from the stone when ripe) and clingstone (the fruit has to be pulled away from the stone when ripe). Most important is that they be grown in a hot, sunny area so sugar develops and the fruit tastes sweet, that they are picked almost dead-ripe. Peaches will appear on the market from late July through September. Most people prefer the late August to early September crop for canning and preserving, as they seem sweetest then. Elberta and Hale are still favorites, although your area may have superior varieties. Check with your local nurserymen or library for information about what grows best locally. Peaches should be checked for color when determining ripeness. The background color should be yellow when they are picked. Some varieties have a pink blush when fully ripe. When you handle a ripe peach, it will feel a little soft. If picked too early, peaches will never get as sweet as they should, and the flesh will be a bit rubbery and not as juicy. Overripe peaches are less sweet, too, so don't pick them either under- or overripe.

Pears

Pears are easy to grow and easy to process. The Bartletts (Bartlett and Red Bartlett) are ready in August and September and are excellent for both eating and canning. (Don't let them get overripe; they ripen from the core out and can be bad before you realize it.) Late fall pears (Anjou, Bosc, Comice, Nelis, Forgue, and Seckel) are primarily for eating or short-cooking, not for canning and processing. (Check with authorities to find what variety is best locally.) Pears do not freeze well—they turn mushy.

This is one fruit which should *not* be allowed to ripen on the tree. Pears should be picked while still firm or they will develop grittiness and the inside will be spoiled, as mentioned. They should just be turning light yellow-green or red (Red Bartlett, Bosc) and the flesh should be slightly soft. If you plan to keep pears before processing, watch them to be sure they don't overripen and store them in the refrigerator.

Pineapple

When pineapples appear on the market at reasonable prices, you may want to buy them for jam or to combine with other fruit for canning. To pick a ripe pineapple, look for a gold color overall (no green on the outside), press lightly against the side to see if it is slightly soft (too soft means overripe), then smell it. Ripe pineapple has a very sweet smell. Last, try to pull out one of the top's inner leaves. If it pulls out easily, the fruit is ripe. Pineapple is usually cheapest in Spring.

Prunes/Plums

Have you ever wondered about the difference between a prune and a plum? The technical definition of a prune-plum is one that can be dried whole without removing the pit and without the fruit fermenting. The French plum is used for California dried prunes, but the Italian prune-plum is found most on the market and grown in many backyards. It is a freestone fruit, making it easy to can. Italian prune-plums are good eaten raw, canned, or made into jam or preserves. They are very sweet and juicy and can even be used to help sweeten less sweet fruit. They are available in late August through September in most areas. Santa Rosa and other red plums are much less sweet and need additional sweetening if canned or used for jams and preserves. These are best eaten raw rather than canned for winter use. If you have a tree of these red plums, or know someone who will share with you, can them with apple-pear juice plus a little lemon juice (1 tablespoon per cup of fruit juice) to get them sweet enough. If making jam, use with sweet apples or other sweet fruit to reduce tartness. Don't let color be the deciding factor. Italian prune-plums should be very dark and slightly soft—but taste them to be sure. Taste is also the best test for red plums. The inside of any plum should be yellowish, rather than green, when you cut into it.

How to Choose Vegetables for Canning and Pickling

Home-grown vegetables are always freshest, but some nearly as good can be bought at farmers' stands or country markets during harvest time. Since most vegetables continue to ripen after they are picked, they should be used immediately or kept refrigerated until used. This won't completely stop the process of ripening, but will slow it down. All vegetables, except tomatoes and pickles, are low acid foods and therefore *must be* canned in a pressure cooker to reach 240 degrees and thus destroy the botulism spores and assure a safe product.

Asparagus

Asparagus is available late April and early May in most areas. Spears should not have overripened so that they are tough and the stems woody. Snap the stem to be sure it is fresh. It will continue to mature after picking, so process or refrigerate at once. (Three to four days shelf life in refrigerator.)

Beans

Green beans are most available in August, limas in late August. Beans should not be too large or they become tough. The best just bulge a little from the seeds inside and green beans should snap easily. Limas should have full, firm pods. Some sizes are deceiving—giant beans may still be very tender even when large. Some don't freeze well. Find out about the varieties and what they are generally used for before you buy them. Your local Extension Agent can supply you with information about what grows best in your area. Stringless varieties may sound superior, but most green beans are stringless if young and tender. Again, process immediately or refrigerate to slow the ripening process.

Beets

Beets are available all summer long; peak season is in August. Pick beets that are not too large, with fresh, unwilted greens. They should feel firm, and the center stem should not be too thick.

Broccoli

Broccoli is at its peak in August. Buds should be tight—never opened and showing yellow. The stem should not be tough and leaves should be a good green. Broccoli should never be limp—it is as crisp and "snappy" as green beans when at its best. Refrigerate if not using or processing immediately. It will keep in the refrigerator for three to five days without wilting badly.

Cabbage

Most cabbage used for pickling and slaw is available in August and early September. Cabbage should look and feel firm, have a good green (or red-purple) color, and feel crisp when you lift an outer leaf. If cabbage has split, it is too ripe. Refrigerate if not using or processing immediately. It will keep in the refrigerator for a week or longer.

Carrots

Carrots are cheapest in August and September. They should be tender, not woody. When they have been in cold storage for many months, they tend to dry out and will not taste as good as fresh. In winter, picking bulk carrots is best; if you look for medium-sized ones, you will probably avoid those with woody centers. Carrots will store well if kept in a cool, somewhat humid place, like a fruit cellar, and will keep for several weeks in the refrigerator.

Cauliflower

Cauliflower is at its peak in August. It should be creamy white. If yellow, it is probably overripe. Bud segments should be firm and tight; leaves should be green and firm. To keep, remove leaves and refrigerate.

Corn

Corn is available from early August through late September in most areas. Be sure you are buying sweet corn (not field corn). The husk should be light green (not yellow) and crisp, with a dark, rather dry tassel. The husk should feel firm. Peel it back and look at the kernels to gauge maturity: light yellow is sweetest; too pale will be immature, too dark will be overripe.

Cucumbers

Pickling size cucumbers are available from mid-August through

September. They should be picked when young and green so seeds are still soft. If cucumbers are yellow, they are too ripe and should be thrown away unless used to make ripe cucumber pickles. (Don't try to eat them when they are yellow.) Cucumbers to be used for small, whole, sweet pickles should be from two to four inches long; for dills, five to six inches long; and for slicing into bread-and-butter pickles or for relishes, six to eight inches long. Discard any over this size, as the seeds will get tough. Refrigerate until used. Cucumbers should be used within twenty-four hours of picking for best quality pickle. Grocery store cucumbers are not suitable for pickling because they have a waxy coating that doesn't allow brine to penetrate.

Mushrooms

Mushrooms are available fresh during most of the year. The freshest have closed caps (brown gills do not show). Be sure they are firm, with no soft spots. Just before using, wash gently under cool water. Avoid bruising, and do not soak in water longer than necessary to remove dirt. Chop or slice stems and use only in long-cooking dishes. Canned mushrooms contain less moisture than fresh. When using them in a recipe that calls for fresh mushrooms, you may need to add two to three tablespoons of the liquid per cup. Wild mushrooms may be used as easily as commercially grown (the variations in moisture content are slight and will not make a difference in cooked dishes), but be sure you have expert identification skills. Every year serious illnesses or deaths are caused by people eating wild mushrooms they thought were safe.

Onions

Onions are available all year long, but are most available in late August and September. Various varieties of onions have differences in flavor. Yellow onions are strongest, while Bermuda-type (Walla Walla Sweets) are milder and a little softer, as are the sweet red onions. It must feel firm. The outer skin should look clean, should show no signs of bruising or mold, and the tops should not be soft, but rather dry with no signs of sprouting. Tiny pickling onions should be white with skins that peel off easily, leaving a firm inside. Red onions will tend to give some red color when cooked with other vegetables. They are recommended primarily for sandwiches and salad use.

Peas

Peas are in season from June through mid-July. Pods should be well-filled and medium green. They should be firm and not wilted. Different varieties will come in varying lengths, but a four-inch pod is probably a good size, provided it is filled out properly. Peas should be shelled and processed immediately, or refrigerated unshelled to keep them from overmaturing and losing their tenderness and sweetness. They will stay fresh for two or three days in the refrigerator. Peas with edible pods should barely show the peas they contain. They should be firm, with no signs of wilt. These peas will lose freshness quickly and should be used within a day or two.

Peppers

Did you know that green peppers are just immature, sweet, red peppers? They are at their peak late in summer, though you can buy them all year. If you are using lots, buy in bulk. They will keep in the refrigerator for several weeks. Peppers should be firm, have no discoloration around the stem, and have a waxy look to the skin. Size is unimportant. They do not toughen as they turn red, so those partly turned are as good as those completely green.

Pumpkins and Winter Squash

Winter squash is available in September and October. Dark green winter squash should not show any really yellow areas; some orange is acceptable. The darker green the better is the rule for some varieties, while others never turn dark green, so you must know what kind you have and what it should look like when mature. Pumpkin should be overall orange. (Do not can mashed pumpkin. Can pumpkin only in cubes.) The skin of both winter squash and pumpkin should be tough, not soft. Winter squash should be cut with a two-inch stem. Let the squash age before you plan to cook it. I usually leave Hubbard-type squash for three weeks to a month to dry before processing for the freezer. Watch to be sure that no water gets on the squash (or pumpkin) since some molds that may form are unhealthy.

Summer Squash (Zucchini, Crook Neck, Scallop)

Summer squash is usually available from mid-July through September. These should be picked when young and tender. Yellow types should be pale yellow, scallop should be greenish-white, and zucchini should be dark green. Summer squash should feel soft if pressed with a fingernail. Hard rind means overripe squash—discard it. Uncut summer squash will keep for five to seven days in the refrigerator.

Tomatoes

Peak season for tomatoes varies with climate, but late August into September is usual. The best tomatoes are ripened on the vine. They should feel firm, look ripe (red and juicy), and smell ripe. You can use your nose to tell you about tomatoes as easily as you can about fruit. Unripe tomatoes will ripen eventually, but they won't taste the same as those ripened before picking. If you want to make green-tomato dishes, buy them hard and green. You'll have to store them in the refrigerator or they will soon be red and ripening. Refrigerate all tomatoes unless using immediately. They will then keep for several days, unless extremely ripe when refrigerated. It is essential that tomatoes used in canning be just ripe. Tomatoes become less acidic as they become overly ripe and may be unsafe when canned like fruit in a water bath canner. Because some tomatoes in Washington and Oregon have been found to be marginally acidic, Washington State University, Oregon State University, and the University of Idaho recommend for the Pacific Northwest that citric acid, U.S.P., or lemon juice be added to tomatoes to assure safety in the final product. For every pint, add ¼ teaspoon citric acid or 1 tablespoon bottled lemon juice. For every quart, add ½ teaspoon citric acid or 2 tablespoons bottled lemon juice.

Equipment You'll Need

For Water Bath or Pressure Cooker Canning

Large nonaluminum kettle, 8 to 10 quart capacity
Large wooden spoon, long-handled
Slotted spoon, long-handled
Colander or wire basket
Large bowls
Measuring cups (1-, 2-, and 4-cup are handy)
Measuring spoons
Paring knife, slicing knife
Large tongs
Water-bath canner, deep enough for jars on rack, plus 2 inches or
        Pressure cooker/canner (8-quart size) with rack*
Tea kettle
Canning jars**
Canning lids with jar rings
Lettuce/salad spinner (optional)

* It is a good idea to have your pressure gauge checked annually for

accuracy. The manufacturer's instruction booklet that comes with your pressure cooker should show where it can be sent for service, or if you live in a large city, you can check the Yellow Pages under "pressure gauges."

** Jars must be canning strength and have lids which can seal with processing. According to Jeanne Lesem's book, *The Pleasures of Preserving and Pickling,* Cornell University's College of Human Ecology approves use of peanut butter and pint and quart mayonnaise jars for food requiring water bath processing. I personally do not and would never recommend the use of jars which were not designed for home canning. For pressure cooker processing, old jars may not stand up under the processing. If a pressure cooker will be used, be safe and buy new canning jars (or like-new jars at the Salvation Army and Goodwill Industries). Be sure they have no chips or cracks, especially along the lips.

For Freezing Fruits and Vegetables

Freezing containers with tight lids*
Plastic bag liners (optional)
Freezer (preferably with sharp freeze unit. Fast freezing gives a more
     tender result. If no sharp freeze is available, freeze smaller amounts
     at a time.)

* I have kept plastic freezing containers for years, using them over and over. If plastic bags are used inside them before adding fruit, they keep the fruit from getting freezer burn and prevent the plastic containers from getting stained or picking up flavors. The regular lock-top plastic bags bought in the grocery store work well. They are not cheap, but they contribute to keeping the frozen fruit in A-1 condition.

Also Needed for Making Jam and Jelly

Jelly jars with sealing lids
Jelly bag (or cheesecloth to make one)

Also Needed for Making Pickles

Food mill, 1-quart size or larger
Meat grinder with various blades
Spice bag (or cloth to improvise one)

How to Sterilize Equipment

To be sure that home-processed foods stay free from bacteria, jars should be sterilized before use. This isn't hard but takes time, so allow for it when you plan your canning and have them ready when needed.

Jars should be clean. Wash them in hot, soapy water and rinse well, or put them in the dishwasher and let it do the work. After cleaning, put them in a deep water bath to boil unless they will be processed again later. Fill the water bath well over half full with hot water. Cover and place over medium heat. (There should be a rack for the jars to sit on so they don't come in direct contact with the bottom of the water bath.) Using tongs, place jars upright in the bath, tilting as you put them in so hot water partially fills them and they stand upright without floating. When the bath is full of jars, add boiling water to cover them by at least one inch. Replace cover and boil for twenty minutes. Have the jars hot to use when the fruit is ready. Don't take them out and leave them in the open air, or they won't be sterile anymore. You must use sterile tongs and take them out as needed to keep them sterile. Place jar rings, lids, and tongs in a smaller pan and cover with boiling water. These need only be boiled five minutes but it doesn't hurt them to boil longer, provided they are covered with water. To be certain, read manufacturers' directions on lids before starting to process. Remove tongs first, and use to take lids and rings out as needed. (Keep all but handle of tongs sterile.)

If you are going to process the filled jars in a boiling water bath or pressure cooker, you still need the jars hot, so put them along with the lids in boiling water to heat, but don't boil.

Preserving with Fruit Juice Sweetening

Canning Fruits

Methods of Processing

There are two ways to pack fruit: hot pack or raw or cold pack. There are advantages and disadvantages to both; you may want to try each before settling on one.

In hot pack canning, place the fruit in a large kettle (nonaluminum is preferred), add sweetening, and cook until tender. Taste the cooked product and add more sweetening, lemon juice, or spices as needed. The hot fruit is then packed into hot, clean jars, liquid is added to within one-half inch of jar rim, lids are added, and the jar is boiled in a water bath (or pressure cooker) to ensure sealing and sterilization. (You cannot safely put fruit into sterile jars and omit this final step because air in the jar needs to be sterilized to prevent bacteria or mold growth. Jar tops must be completely covered with boiling water all the time they are processing. In the pressure cooker jars are processed only long enough to ensure sealing.)

The raw or cold pack method is simpler, quicker, and saves having a dirty kettle, but does not give you a chance to taste the cooked product or make any changes in ingredients, once cooked. In this case, pack peeled (sliced if desired) fruit directly into hot, clean jars, add liquid to within one-half inch from top of jar, screw on hot jar lids, and put into boiling water bath or pressure cooker to process. Liquid must be added to the fruit to help the cooking process. Heat is slow to penetrate solids and liquid helps spread the heat as well as adding some sweetness to the fruit.

Prepare a small batch of each fruit using the hot pack method to see how much sweetening or other flavoring is needed. Then go ahead and use the raw or cold pack method for the rest of the batch.

What to Do First

Choose a fruit combination(s). Using the following Trial Batch Recipe, check to see if they really taste good. If they do but you'd like them sweeter, adjust the sweetening by trying other juices or more concentrated juices (undiluted, possibly). White grape juice gives the sweetest taste; try using that or concentrated apple juice.

Trial Batch Recipe

Chopped fruit   1 cup peeled with blossom and stem removed
Selected syrup   ¼ cup (see directions in this section)
Lemon juice   ¼ teaspoon
Salt   dash (optional)

Place fruit in saucepan, add syrup, lemon juice, and salt. Cover and simmer for 8 to 10 minutes or until fruit is soft. Remove from heat, allow to cool before tasting. Add spice(s) if desired. Return to heat for 2 to 3 minutes to allow flavor to partly penetrate the fruit. Cool before tasting. Makes 1 cup.

Once you have tried a batch and are sure it is what you want, proceed with cold pack canning without worrying about the end product.

Preparing Fruit for Canning or Freezing

Pick over fruit to select ripe, unbruised pieces. (Set aside bruised pieces for use in preserves or jam.) Wash in cold water to remove dirt or spray. If fruit is to be peeled, prepare a boiling water bath and a cold water bath. Do only a few pieces at a time, dropping each into boiling water for about one minute, then into cold. This will normally loosen skins so they can be peeled off quickly. When fruit is peeled, drop into a bowl into which you have added two tablespoons lemon juice to cold water (three tablespoons lemon juice for soft fruit). Keep fruit pieces covered with this liquid to prevent browning until ready to use. (You can reuse the liquid by refrigerating and adding more lemon juice the second day. It can then be used as liquid for fruit syrup.)

When processing berries, simply wash in cold water, then pick over to remove leaves, stems, or debris. Dry thoroughly on layers of absorbent towels, or in a lettuce spinner, in small batches. If whole strawberries are to be canned or frozen, prick each with a fork so the liquid (or cold) will penetrate the berry quickly.

Choosing and Making the Syrup

All these syrups contain fruit juice (or honey), water, and lemon juice. (The recipes in the first section use only fruit juice.) Lemon juice helps preserve color and enhances natural sweetness. No matter which syrup you decide to try, you'll need a large kettle of boiling water, plus a supply of pure lemon juice.

The sweetening required to enhance each fruit varies with each year's crop. Because of this, it is not possible to give exact directions. The suggested juice-fruit combinations are the ones I liked best the year I tried them. Each year, prepare a trial batch for each fruit. Remember, canned fruit tastes less sweet than fresh if no sweetening is added. Using the fruit's natural juice for sweetening will give the truest flavor but may not be sweet enough.

On the following pages you will find suggested dilutions of various juices. *Make only one to two quarts liquid at one time,* preparing more if needed. This way you won't waste any if you change your mind about what to use. If you have the kettle boiling and your other ingredients handy, it only takes a minute to combine them. How much do you need? In general, between one-fourth and one-third cup syrup per half-pint jar, or between one and one and one-third cups for a quart, if you have the fruit really packed in, as already suggested. Roughly measure the amount of fruit to be canned (a quart-sized measuring cup is handy for this), and *prepare about one quart liquid for every three quarts fruit measured.*

Syrups for Sweetening

No-Added-Sweetener Syrup: For each cup boiled water, add one to one and one-half teaspoons lemon juice (depending upon how tart the fruit is; use the higher amount for sweet fruit), plus a dash of salt (optional) to help bring out the natural flavor. Leave in (or add) a few fruit pits to add flavor.

Fruit-Juice Sweetened Syrup: Use apple juice (regular or concentrated), white grape juice, pineapple, orange, or any combined juices such as apple/pear, orange/pineapple, etc. To be sure you like the combination you have selected, make only a very small amount of the syrup and try the Trial Batch Recipe. (I cannot emphasize this enough—try before you do a big batch!)

Artificially Sweetened Syrup: I have not included directions for canning and preserving with artificial sweeteners, as this is completely covered in my dietetic cookbook, *How to Have Your Cake—and Eat It, Too!* available from your bookseller or from Alaska Northwest Publishing, Box 4EEE, Anchorage, Alaska 99509.

Directions for Syrup made with Natural Juice

*Light Syrup**

⅓ cup apple juice plus 1 teaspoon lemon juice plus boiled water
    equals 1 cup syrup
¼ cup white grape juice plus 1 teaspoon lemon juice plus boiled water
    equals 1 cup syrup
⅓ cup pineapple juice plus 1 teaspoon lemon juice plus boiled water
    equals 1 cup syrup
⅓ cup apple-pear juice plus 1 teaspoon lemon juice plus boiled water
    equals 1 cup syrup

½ cup orange juice plus 1 teaspoon lemon juice plus boiled water
   equals 1 cup syrup

*Medium Syrup**

⅔ cup apple juice plus 1¼ teaspoons lemon juice plus boiled water
   equals 1 cup syrup
½ cup white grape juice plus 1½ teaspoons lemon juice plus boiled water
   equals 1 cup syrup
⅔ cup pineapple juice plus 1 teaspoon lemon juice plus boiled water
   equals 1 cup syrup
⅔ cup apple-pear juice plus 1 teaspoon lemon juice plus boiled water
   equals 1 cup syrup
1 cup orange juice (less 1 teaspoon) plus 1 teaspoon lemon juice equals
   1 cup syrup

*Heavy Syrup**

½ cup concentrated apple juice (frozen) plus 1½ teaspoons lemon juice
   plus boiled water equals 1 cup syrup
1 cup white grape juice (less 2 teaspoons) plus 2 teaspoons lemon juice
   equals 1 cup syrup
½ cup concentrated pineapple juice (frozen) plus 1½ teaspoons lemon
   juice plus boiled water equals 1 cup syrup

We do not recommend heavy syrup. The concentrated fruit juice over-
powers the natural taste of the fruit.
* All of these syrups are less sweet than those made with sugar.

Hot Pack Canning Method

Select a large, nonaluminum kettle, with at least two and one-half
times the volume you plan to can (stainless steel is good, but watch for
sticking). Place peeled, chopped, or otherwise prepared fruit in kettle,
measuring volume to know how much syrup to add. For each quart of
fruit, add one cup syrup. Place over medium heat and, when boiling, turn
down to low. Cook ten to fifteen minutes or longer, until fruit is soft. Skim
if necessary. While this cooks, prepare jars in boiling water. Place lids and
screw caps in separate pan and cover with hot water (keep boiling until
ready to use). When fruit is ready, drain jars, using sterile tongs to avoid
contaminating them with your hands.

Pack fruit firmly into jars. Use a sterile spoon-end or knife handle,
but don't squash any pieces. Slices pack best and require least syrup.
Leave at least one inch at top of jar for expansion when cooking. Pour hot

fruit liquid over packed fruit, using spoon or knife-end on each side to be sure there are no air pockets in the jar. Cap with sterile lid; screw down firmly. Place in boiling water bath (or in pressure cooker) to process for secure sealing. Jars must be well covered with water for entire boiling—add more boiling water if necessary during cooking.

Note: Only acid fruits are safe processed in a boiling water bath. All others must be done in a pressure cooker. The following are safe to process in a water bath: apples, apricots, apple-berry mixtures, berries, peaches, pears, nectarines, pineapple, plums, rhubarb, and tomatoes (with lemon juice added to be sure they are acid enough).

Although sugar is a preservative, there is not enough sugar, even in a heavy syrup, to act totally as a preservative. It is the acid in combination with vacuum canning that preserves fruit. If you plan to alter a recipe by removing sugar, be sure to add lemon juice or other acid.

Table 2, Processing Time for Hot Pack Fruits, should be your guide when timing the boiling water bath. A table of nutritional values for these fruits will be found in the Appendix.

Raw or Cold Pack Canning Method

This is a time-saving method, once you determine what to use for sweetening. Make a stove-top Trial Batch (see Index). Each fruit requires different handling, so individual instructions are provided. A boiling water bath for jars and lids is required for all. Nutritional values for fruits processed according to these directions may be found in the Appendix.

Applesauce: This cannot be made cold pack. You must do it hot pack and then process by water bath or pressure cooker or freeze to preserve it. For each cup apples (quartered, blossom and stem ends removed), add ¼ cup apple juice (use concentrated apple juice if fruit is very tart). Cover, cook very slowly until soft and mushy. You can mash the fruit with a potato masher to break up chunks if you want to hurry the cooking. When very soft, remove from heat and put through food mill or colander to remove skins and other coarse pieces. Season with lemon juice (at least 1 tablespoon per quart applesauce) and spices. First measure pureed sauce, then add lemon juice, mixing well. To this try adding up to ¼ teaspoon cinnamon, ⅛ teaspoon nutmeg, and 1/16 teaspoon ginger per cup of sauce. Mix well and taste, then reheat. Put in clean, hot jars, leaving ½ inch headspace, and top with hot lids, screwed down firmly. Place in boiling water bath or pressure cooker and cook according to times listed in Table 2.

Apple Slices: Peel, core, and slice apples, placing in bowl of cold water containing 1½ tablespoons lemon juice per pint to prevent browning.

Table 2
Processing Time for Hot Pack Fruits
(timing begins after water reboils, jars completely covered with liquid)

Fruit	Minutes for Boiling Water Bath		Minutes for Pressure Cooker (at 5 pounds pressure) Pint and Quart
	Pint	Quart	
Applesauce	10	10	8
Apple Slices	15	20	10
Apricots	20	25	10
Berry/Applesauce	10	10	8
Berries	10	15	8
Cherries	10	15	9
Nectarines (halves)	20	25	10
Peaches (halves)	20	25	10
Pears (halves)	20	25	9
Pineapple	15	Unknown	8
Plums	20	25	10
Mixed Fruits	20	25	10

Note: Almost as much time is required here as for raw or cold pack fruit because it takes just as long for heat to build up inside the jar when fruit is already cooked—much more time than just cooking the fruit takes. The heat is what kills bacteria; the jar must reach a high internal temperature for the process to be effective.

When ready to pack, drain into a colander (save and reuse liquid). Pack into hot jars, leaving 1 inch at top. Use end of spoon or knife to be sure there are no air pockets among slices. Taste them to see how sweet they are. If quite sweet, use light syrup; otherwise, medium syrup. Syrup with an apple juice base is the best choice. Add syrup, cap with hot lids, and screw down tightly. Process in boiling water bath 25 minutes after boiling starts, or in pressure cooker for 10 minutes at 5 pounds pressure.

Apricots: These can be processed peeled or unpeeled. To peel, drop (a few at a time) into boiling water for 1 minute, then into cold water. If ripe, the skin should slip off readily. Use light or medium syrup, depending upon which is needed. Some apricots are very sweet (Tilton and Moorpack), others are more tart. Always taste before buying a quantity for canning. Diluted apple juice is best for syrup sweetening. Be sure to add lemon juice as directed or the apricots will taste flat. Cut the apricots in half, or in quarters if large. Pack directly into clean, hot jars, leaving as little space as you can. Pour in syrup, leaving ¾ inch at top. Cap with hot lids, screwed down tightly. Process in boiling water bath 25 minutes for pints or 30 minutes for quarts after water has returned to boiling, or in pressure cooker for 10 minutes at 5 pounds pressure.
Note: A pit or two left in each jar will give a mild almond flavor. Add a slice of lemon peel as well for an interesting combination of flavors.

Combine apricots with sliced apples to make the fruit go further. Use an equal amount of fairly ripe, early Yellow Transparent or Lodi apples. These varieties are so mild that they will not overpower the apricot taste. Prepare slices as directed earlier in this chapter, then combine with quartered apricots in equal amounts (or ⅓ apples and ⅔ apricots). Pack and process as for apricots alone.

Berries: Berries vary in sweetness almost more than any other fruit. Pick them fresh and ripe for best results. Pick over berries, removing overripe or bruised fruit. Wash and dry before packing in clean, hot jars. Do not mash berries, but pack as full as you can without crushing fruit, leaving 1 inch at top for expansion during cooking. If you are canning whole strawberries, prick each with a fork before placing into the jars so the liquid can penetrate the berry. The following berry-syrup combinations work well together:

Boysenberries	White grape juice, medium syrup, extra lemon juice.
Loganberries	White grape juice, medium syrup, extra lemon juice.
Raspberries	Apple juice, medium syrup.

Strawberries	Apple-pear juice, medium syrup.
Wild Blackberries	White grape juice, medium syrup, extra lemon juice.
Blueberries	White grape juice, medium syrup, extra lemon juice.
Huckleberries	White grape juice, medium syrup, extra lemon juice.

You may prefer other combinations—try a sample batch before you pack to save having fruit you don't enjoy eating and to allow adjustment for the change in fruit from year to year. Heat selected syrup; when boiling, cover berries and cap with hot lids, firmly screwed down. Process in boiling water bath for 15 minutes after water returns to boiling, or in pressure cooker for 8 minutes at 5 pounds pressure.

Note: Berries tend to fade when canned. The presence of refined sugar helps prevent this; if refined sugar isn't used, syrup will be quite colorful but the berries will fade. To prevent pale fruit (or actually, to cover the fading), you may add ¼ teaspoon red food coloring to each cup of syrup, or use beet liquid (see Index).

Berry-Applesauce: Among the most delightful combinations of fruit are apple-berry mixtures: boysenberry with apple, raspberry with apple, and strawberry with apple are all so good that one of the top commercial canners makes them for the quality restaurant trade. Do try them; they extend the berry flavor with an inexpensive and tasty apple base. To make these combinations, prepare applesauce as directed earlier in this section, but do not add spices. At this point, set aside applesauce until berry puree is ready.

For berry puree, place berries in large saucepan, including ¼ cup white grape juice for each 2 cups berries. Cover and cook slowly over low heat until berries are very soft. Place in food mill and sieve to remove most of the seeds. Combine equal amounts pureed applesauce and pureed berries. Taste and add lemon juice and/or lemon rind for flavor. Start with 2 teaspoons per quart of berry-applesauce, adding more if needed. If you decide to use red vegetable food coloring, or beet liquid, start with a few drops and add gradually, mixing well after each addition. Overcolored berry-applesauce is not attractive.

When the mixture is ready for processing, pack in clean, hot jars, and cap with hot lids, tightened down firmly. Process in boiling water bath for 20 minutes after water returns to boiling, or in pressure cooker for 10 minutes at 5 pounds pressure. Store in cool, dark place to avoid further fading.

Note: This is delicious with chicken, turkey, pork, or veal. Try it for a change on Thanksgiving in place of cranberry jelly.

Cherries: Wash and dry fruit. Remove stems and pits (buy a cherry-pitter at a kitchen supply store). Place pitted fruit in bowl to save juice. (Work over a bowl when pitting, too.) You don't have to use a lemon-water bath to prevent browning with cherries, so when you have enough ready, start packing jars. More colorful and tastier light cherries will result if a few dark ones are included in the jar. Including a few pits will also add to the flavor.

Light cherries, use medium syrup made from apple or white grape juice. Be sure to use lemon as directed. Pack into clean, hot jars, leaving 1 inch at top. Top with hot lids, firmly screwed down. Process in boiling water bath 25 minutes after boiling starts, or in pressure cooker for 10 minutes at 5 pounds pressure.

Dark cherries, use very light syrup unless cherries are not as sweet as usual. White grape juice or apple-based syrup is tasty; try apple-pear as well. Pack into hot jars, cap and process as for light cherries. A few pits left in the jar greatly add to the flavor. Plan to save and freeze some choice dark cherries for use in fruit cocktail later in the season.

Grapes: Grapes are so available and tasty year-round, most people don't bother canning them. If you want to try it, here are the directions.

Wash grapes, removing stems, dry, pack into clean, hot jars, and cover with boiling syrup. (Medium syrup using white grape juice as the base gives best results.) Top jars with hot lids, tightly screwed down. Place in boiling water bath for 15 minutes after water returns to boiling or in pressure cooker for 12 minutes at 5 pounds pressure. When canning large grapes, prick each before you pack them. This will help heat penetrate the grapes and cook them more evenly.

Nectarines: If you haven't discovered the delicious taste of a ripe nectarine, you have missed some good eating. Nectarines must be soft and ripe to be sweet, and if canned or frozen while hard, they will not be good for anything. Unlike some fruits, they smell good even when not truly ripe, so check each piece to be sure it is ready for processing.

To prepare, dip in boiling water for 1 minute, then in cold water. The skin will slip off easily. Cut into halves or slices, saving a few pits to add for flavor. Pack immediately into jars and cover with syrup quickly to avoid darkening. I like them canned in orange or pineapple juice. Use undiluted orange juice for all the syrup or try a medium syrup pineapple mixture. Make a trial batch and decide which you prefer. You can pack nectarines in halves, but slices give a sweeter product. Pack fruit into clean, hot jars as you prepare it, and add juice/syrup to within 1 inch of the top. Cap with hot lids, screwed down firmly. Process in boiling water bath 20 minutes for slices or 25 minutes for halves after water returns to boiling, or in pressure cooker for 10 minutes at 5 pounds pressure. Nectarines may be included in the fruits used for fruit cocktail. (Use in smaller amounts than peaches or pears; half as much makes a good mixture.)

Peaches: Peaches may all smell good when ripe, but flavor varies greatly from one variety to another. Select those that taste extra good—flavorful and sweet. Save a few peach pits to include in each jar for added flavor. Syrup made with white grape juice or pineapple juice is good; apple juice can also be used, but it does not add as much to the flavor. Most peaches require medium syrup to taste sweet. Peel by dipping in boiling water, then in cold. The skin should slip right off. Pack slices or halves directly into clean, hot jars, catching juice and adding to jars as you pack. Be sure the fruit is packed firmly without mashing it. Cover with hot syrup, leaving ¾ to 1 inch at the top. Cap with hot lids, firmly screwed down. Process in boiling water bath 20 minutes for slices or 25 minutes for halves after water returns to boiling, or in pressure cooker 10 minutes at 5 pounds pressure. Peaches can be spiced or pickled (see Index). To add spice, drop several whole cloves in each jar and/or break up cinnamon sticks and include at least two pieces in the bottom of each jar. Process as usual. Broken pieces of fruit can be set aside for use in jam. Cover with pineapple juice to prevent browning until you can use them—and, of course, keep them in the refrigerator!

Pears: Pears must be eating-ripe. I like Bartletts for canning, but other varieties are good, too. Pears blend well with most other fruits. Use medium syrup made from apple juice, apple-pear juice, white grape juice, or pineapple juice. For the most natural flavor, use apple-pear juice. Dip pears in boiling water for not more than 30 seconds, then into cold. The skin should peel off easily. (If you leave it too long in boiling water, some of the skin color may stay on the pear and it will not look very appetizing.) Remove the core, blossom end, and any fibers. Pack in halves or slices (slices will taste sweeter) directly into hot jars, using a bowl to catch the juice lost as you work, returning it to the jar along with the fruit. Cover with syrup, leaving ¾ to 1 inch at top for expansion. Cover with clean, hot lids screwed down firmly. Process in boiling water bath 15 minutes for slices or 20 minutes for halves after water returns to boiling, or in pressure cooker for 10 minutes at 5 pounds pressure.
Note: Pears can be prepared for salad or garnish use by adding food coloring and/or spices. Make minted pears by adding green food color and mint extract to syrup just before pouring into jars (3 to 4 drops green color and ⅛ to ¼ teaspoon mint flavor per cup syrup). Do the same thing with red color or beet liquid and cinnamon. Make a small test batch to

determine how much flavoring to add.

Pineapple: If you are fortunate enough to have access to tree-ripened pineapple, by all means can your own, but it is not economical to buy at usual retail prices and then can; it is far cheaper to buy already canned in juice. The best syrup is additional pineapple juice—either full strength or diluted half with water—plus 1 teaspoon lemon juice for each cup syrup. Peel the ripe pineapple, removing eyes and cutting out the core. Cut into chunks and pack directly into clean, hot jars. (Be sure to use a bowl to catch any juice lost as you work. It should be added to the syrup and included in the jar as part of the liquid.) Cover with syrup, leaving ¾ to 1 inch at top of jar for expansion. Cover with hot lids, screwed down firmly. Process in boiling water bath for 20 minutes after water has returned to boiling, or in pressure cooker for 10 minutes after pressure reaches 5 pounds.

Small pieces of pineapple can be saved in a covered jar with pineapple juice to keep them fresh. They will last several days in the refrigerator until you can get to making jam or preserves. Pineapple blends well with all types of fruit and the juice prevents browning by preventing oxidation.

Purple Plums: Plums you plan to can should be sweet and soft. Hard, sour plums will make miserable canned fruit. Both apple juice and white grape juice make good medium syrups for purple plums. Try a small batch to see which you prefer before starting. Do not peel plums, but prick them with a fork if you plan to leave them whole. This will help the canning liquid penetrate the fruit so it cooks completely. If canning them whole, merely pack washed fruit into clean, hot jars, filling as full as you can without mashing the fruit. If you want a sweeter product, cut into halves or quarters (if large). Cover with medium-strength hot syrup, leaving ¾ to 1 inch at the top for expansion. Leave a few pits in each jar for added flavor. Cap jars with hot lids, firmly screwed down. Process in boiling water bath for 25 minutes after water returns to boiling, or in pressure cooker for 10 minutes at 5 pounds pressure.

Mixed Fruit (Fruit Cocktail): The usual fruit cocktail mixture combines peaches, pears, pineapple, and green grapes with maraschino cherries for color. Make this combination when peaches and pears are ripe; if you saved some dark cherries, use them for color. The simplest method is to buy chunk-style pineapple packed in its own juice and use it as the base, adding peeled, sliced peaches, peeled pear slices, seedless green grapes, and dark sweet cherries for color and taste. Use a large can of chunk-style pineapple (16 ounces) to make 2 quarts fruit cocktail. Try adding 2 cups each peach slices, pear slices, and ½ cup sweet cherries. Start with 1 cup green grapes, adding more if desired. Include 1 cup nectarines, if desired. Place in a large bowl and try some to see if the mixture suits you. If not, add more of whatever you think lacking. Try using blueberries (sparingly; they may color the syrup), orange and grapefruit sections. Other berries may taste fine, but won't look as good.

For syrup, use the pineapple juice-water-lemon mixture as given in the section on syrup, or try the white grape juice-water-lemon combination. Whichever you select, use medium syrup, including any juice saved from the fruit as you prepared it. If you have no sweet cherries to add, it won't taste much different, but will be less colorful. Red seedless grapes can be substituted, if you can find them; cut the large, red grapes in half if you wish. Mix fruit so varieties are evenly distributed. Pack into clean, hot jars, add hot syrup, leaving 1 inch at top of jar for expansion. Cap with hot lids, screwed down firmly. Process in boiling water bath for 20 minutes after water returns to boiling, or in pressure cooker for 10 minutes at 5 pounds pressure.

How to Check the Seal

You'll be doing at least two types of processing: filling jars or containers with raw or cooked material to be processed in a water bath or pressure cooker. Fruit *must be processed* to keep safely. It's important to check the seal after processing, whichever method you use. When food is packed boiling hot and the jar is to seal itself, you should allow it to stand until room temperature before you test the seal. If the seal is a vacuum-type, check it by pressing the center of the lid. If the lid is down, and does not move when you press, the jar is sealed.

After food is processed in a water bath or pressure cooker, jars should be removed with tongs, then allowed to stand upright until cool. If you hear a popping noise as it cools, a good vacuum is in that jar—just what you want. If the seal has not worked as it should, you either have to keep the food in the refrigerator and use it quickly or reheat it to the boiling point and start over with clean (or sterile) jars and new lids. (Reprocessing means overcooking—less appetizing and attractive.) But if the jars do not have nicks in the edges of the lips and the lids are new, there should not be many which fail to seal when processed properly.

Storing Canned Fruit

Fruit canned without sugar tends to fade, as mentioned before. To help retain the color, keep it in a dark cupboard. (Light speeds up the bleaching process.) Ideal storage would be in a cupboard with doors, or on covered shelves (newspaper works for covering) in a cool basement. Ideal storage temperature is 60 degrees or slightly cooler. Care must be taken that fruit does not freeze, as it will have to be used at once when it thaws, or be discarded. You could recan it in new jars and lids but it won't end up very attractive after double cooking.

If canned fruit smells peculiarly or has mold or other discoloration when you open the jar—discard it. Botulism is not usually found in fruit, but improperly canned fruit could be harmful. Never take chances when it comes to home-canned foods which look suspicious. The Botulin toxin thrives in low-acid foods in an airless environment (like a sealed canning jar).

Freezing Fruits

Most fruits can be frozen successfully, without sugar, if processed properly. Blanching or steaming (to stop the ripening process) is not needed with soft fruits (apricots, peaches, pears, etc.) as it is with vegetables. Dipping fruit in boiling water is not meant as a cooking procedure, but merely helps remove skin without losing any fruit pulp. If fruit is kept at sufficiently low temperatures (0 to 10 degrees F.), enzyme action changing the texture and flavor will be stopped. To prevent discoloration by exposure to oxygen, use a syrup which contains citric acid or ascorbic acid (lemon juice supplies this vitamin C). There doesn't have to be sugar in the syrup. Directions for making it are in the syrup preparation section (see Index).

If you wish to use one of the citric/ascorbic mixtures on the market (Fruit-Fresh, etc.) instead of plain lemon juice, use as directed on package, adding before fruit is added to liquid. Add after liquid has been heated (if necessary) and pack fruit directly into it, pouring over fruit as fast as it is packed into containers. It prevents darkening from air exposure but won't remove the dark color once it has developed.

Some fruits do well frozen whole—cherries and berries, for example. They don't need any syrup or other treatment, but they must be well wrapped after freezing to prevent freezer burn and dehydration. They are the easiest to process and taste so good later on. Check the following chart to see what the fruit you are planning to use will require.

Fruits Which Can Be Frozen Without Syrup

Blueberries*
Boysenberries
Cranberries
Currants
Himalayan Blackberries
Loganberries
Melons
Pineapple

Raspberries
Rhubarb
Sweet Cherries, pitted or with
    stems left on
Strawberries, sliced or whole
    (prick with fork to allow air
    release)

Use only tree-ripened fruit, ready to eat. Wash and dry (or use a lettuce spinner to remove surplus water). Place individual pieces on cookie sheet and sharp freeze until hard. Pack into plastic bags or boxes with tight lids. To protect against freezer burn, place several small bags inside a larger one and secure tightly. Pack only enough for one meal in each container as fruit is best used immediately after thawing.
* Blanch blueberries with steam for 1 minute to keep skins tender. Chill before freezing.

Fruits Which Need Dipping Before Freezing

Apple slices
Plums, pitted

Use only tree-ripened fruit. Wash, dry well, then dip into solution of 1½ tablespoons lemon juice (or ⅛ teaspoon ascorbic acid) in 2 cups of cold water. Drain well (or use lettuce spinner), freeze on cookie sheets until hard. Package in tightly covered containers, freeze in sharp section of freezer, removing to other storage after 1 hour.
Note: You can freeze these fruits in the syrup you used for dipping. Be sure fruit is under the syrup so the exposed section doesn't turn dark.

Fruits Best Frozen in Syrup/Juice

Apricots
Grapefruit sections
Grapes
Melons

Nectarines
Orange sections
Peaches
Pears

Use only tree-ripened fruit. Wash, dry well, pack into sturdy containers, cover with syrup of your choice, leaving 1 inch at top for expansion, cover tightly, and place in sharp freeze section of freezer until hard. To remove skins before freezing, dip washed fruit into boiling water for 1 minute, then into cold. If the fruit is really ripe, the skin should slip off easily. Cover with syrup and freeze as directed. Use the same juices for freezing as for canning.

Choosing and Preparing Fruit for Freezing

Freeze fruit in pure juice, adding two teaspoons lemon juice per cup to prevent discoloring, or in medium syrup made with fruit juice as described in the syrup preparation section (see Index). I recommend using medium syrup or pure juice plus lemon juice for best flavor. Don't discard the liquid from frozen fruit—eat it along with the fruit. The same combinations you liked fresh will do well frozen. Try a small batch to see if you like fruit which has been frozen—some people don't. You may prefer apricots, peaches, and pears canned.

Apples: Wash, peel, and core. Cut into ⅛-inch slices and drop into lemon water until ready to freeze (3 tablespoons lemon juice per 2 cups water). Pack into rigid containers, leaving 1 inch at top. Cover all fruit with medium apple juice syrup to within ¾ inch of top. Place lids on containers. Cover. Freeze immediately. To use, allow to thaw in container or in colander so liquid can drain into bowl. Use liquid in puddings or other dishes made with the fruit.

Applesauce: Prepare according to your own recipe or see Index for directions. Pack into rigid containers, leaving ¾-inch space at top. Cover tightly, freeze immediately. To use, thaw in container in refrigerator overnight.

Apricots: (I prefer canning these unless the fruit is especially sweet.) Wash and cut in half, removing pits. Pack into rigid containers, covering with medium apple juice or white grape juice syrup to within ¾ inch of top. Freeze immediately. To use, thaw overnight in container in refrigerator or in colander so liquid can drain into bowl.

Blueberries: Discard soft or damaged berries. Wash well, place in lettuce spinner or on paper towels to dry. Spread on cookie sheets, place in sharp freeze section of freezer. Cover with foil or plastic wrap. When hard, pour frozen fruit into covered plastic containers. To use, thaw overnight in container in refrigerator or use unthawed in fresh fruit cup for texture variety.

Sweet Cherries and Seedless Grapes: Discard bruised cherries or grapes. Wash, stem, pit, and dry. Pack in rigid containers, cover with light white grape juice syrup to within ¾ inch of top. Cover. Freeze. To use, thaw in container in colander. Use liquid with fruit in making puddings or other desserts.

Orange and/or Grapefruit Sections: To save money on citrus fruit, pack it when the season's peak arrives. Peel and section fruit, removing pits and white membrane. Save juice lost as you are sectioning and add to juice for freezing. Pack into rigid containers, leaving ¾ inch at top, cover with undiluted orange or grapefruit juice. Cover. Freeze. To use, thaw in container overnight in refrigerator. Serve in juice.

Peaches and Nectarines: Wash fruit, blanch 1 minute in boiling water, then in cold. Skin should slip off easily. Halve or slice, removing pits. Pack into rigid containers, leaving ¾ inch at top; cover with undiluted orange juice. Be sure fruit is covered to prevent browning. Cover. Freeze. To use, thaw overnight in container in refrigerator. Serve in juice.

Pears: (I prefer canning unless fruit is to be used partly frozen.) Wash fruit, drop in boiling water for 1 minute, then in cold water to remove skin. Use dull side of knife to gently scrape off any discolorations. Halve or slice to remove seeds and stem. Heat apple-pear juice syrup (light or medium depending upon sweetness of fruit). Drop in pears and poach for about 2 minutes. Drain syrup and allow to cool. Pack into rigid containers, leaving ¾ inch at top. Pour cooled liquid over fruit to prevent browning. Cover. Freeze. To use, thaw overnight in container in refrigerator. Serve in syrup. May be used when still partly frozen as ingredient in fresh fruit cup.

Plums: Plums may be frozen in halves, to be eaten like fresh fruit, without any processing. Wash, pit, and remove stems, then place cut side down on cookie sheets and sharp freeze. When hard, place in freezer bags or rigid containers, cover and store. To use, thaw only enough to soften slightly. Eat while still firm.

Plums may also be frozen in medium syrup (apple or white grape juice) if they are to be cooked when thawed (in puddings, etc.). Place halves in rigid container; cover with medium syrup, leaving ¾ inch at top; add lid, and freeze immediately. To use, thaw in colander, saving liquid for use in puddings or other cooking, or serve in juice.

Raspberries, Boysenberries, Loganberries, etc.: Wash and dry berries (with lettuce spinner or on paper towels). Place on cookie sheet, and sharp freeze. When hard, place in heavy freezing plastic bags or in rigid containers with tight lids. To use, thaw in containers, serve liquid with fruit or save for cooking. Try the berries still partly frozen in fruit cup and other mixed fruit dishes.

To freeze berries in liquid, use light apple juice syrup. Cover berries completely, leaving ¾ inch at top, cover container and sharp freeze. Thaw overnight in container in refrigerator. Serve with liquid. (They will be slightly more tender frozen in liquid than when frozen dry.)

Rhubarb: Freezing rhubarb is simple. Wash and dry the stalks, cut them into suitable pieces (½ inch), pack them into firm, covered containers or heavy freezing bags, cover and freeze. To use, thaw in colander or overnight in refrigerator. Add some form of sweetening when cooking rhubarb. This can be apple juice (concentrated to give most sweetening), apples plus apple juice, strawberries plus white grape juice, or any other combination. It is difficult to get rhubarb sweet enough without combining with another sweeter fruit. Try small batches of various combinations. Adding lemon juice helps to bring out the natural sweetness of any fruit and rhubarb is no exception. You may want as much as 1 tablespoon per cup cooked rhubarb—start with less and taste as you add.

Strawberries: Strawberries can be frozen whole (prick with fork) or in halves. When frozen whole, no syrup is needed. Wash berries, dry well (lettuce spinner or paper towels), then place on cookie sheets to sharp freeze. When frozen, place in heavy plastic bags or rigid containers with tight tops. If cut into halves, berries are best frozen in syrup. Place washed, cut, and dried berries in rigid containers, leaving ¾ inch at top. Cover with light apple or white grape juice syrup, leaving ¾ inch at top. Place lid on container and freeze immediately. To use, thaw in colander, saving liquid to be used with fruit in cooking or eaten with the berries.

Mixed Fruits: Prepare mixed fruit as directed for canning. Instead of jars, put in rigid freezing containers, leaving ¾ inch at top. Add medium white grape juice syrup, being sure to completely cover all fruit to prevent browning. Freeze at once. To use, thaw overnight in refrigerator. Serve in juice.

Freezing Vegetables

Vegetables do not require sugar or other sweetening when frozen (canned peas, corn, and succotash are usually sweetened when canned). It is very easy to freeze vegetables; the following directions are simple and the results will be well worth your time. Some vegetables do not freeze well. Those listed, however, are excellent frozen.

Asparagus: Wash; cut stems approximately 5 inches from tip. (You may cut slices from the lower portion down as far as it cuts easily. These can be frozen separately and used as a base for excellent asparagus soup.) Blanch in boiling water for 5 to 7 minutes after water returns to boiling. Drain, chill in ice water for 5 minutes. Drain (a lettuce spinner works very well), pack in plastic freezer bags or boxes. Sharp freeze. To use, remove from freezer just before cooking. *Do not thaw*. Steaming is recommended.

Beans: String beans should be washed, strings removed, and cut into pieces of the size you prefer. Blanch in boiling water bath for 2 minutes after water returns to boiling. Drain, chill in ice water for 5 minutes. Drain well, pack in plastic freezer bags or boxes. Sharp freeze. To use, remove from freezer just before cooking. *Do not thaw*. Steaming is recommended.

Lima and Shell beans should be shelled, then blanched in boiling water bath for 1½ minutes after water returns to boiling. Drain, chill in ice water for 4 minutes. Drain well, pack in plastic freezer bags or boxes. Sharp freeze. To use, remove from freezer just before cooking. *Do not thaw*. Steaming is recommended.

Broccoli: Broccoli can be processed whole by splitting the stems, or chopped into pieces. If using whole broccoli, trim the stems to 5 inches from the top. Split stems so the pieces are not more than ½ inch thick. Soak in lightly salted water for 15 minutes to remove any insects. Drain, blanch in boiling water bath for 3 minutes after water returns to boiling. Drain, chill in ice water for 5 minutes, then drain well. Pack in plastic freezer bags or boxes. Sharp freeze. To use, remove from freezer just before cooking. *Do not thaw*. Steaming is recommended.

Cauliflower: Remove leaves, cut off bottom stem, and separate into flowerlets. Wash, drain, blanch in boiling water bath for 3 minutes after water returns to boiling. Drain, chill in ice water for 4 minutes. Drain well, pack in plastic freezer bags or boxes. Sharp freeze. To use, remove from freezer just before cooking. *Do not thaw*. Steaming is recommended.

Peas: Both shelled peas and peas with edible pods can be frozen successfully. Shell peas, blanch in boiling water bath for 1½ minutes after water returns to boiling. Drain, chill in ice water for 3 minutes. Drain well, pack in plastic freezer bags or boxes. Sharp freeze. To use, remove from freezer just before cooking. *Do not thaw*. Steaming is recommended.

Peapods are prepared by removing the stem and blossom end. Wash, drain, blanch in boiling water bath for 30 seconds after water returns to boiling. Drain immediately, chill in ice water for 4 minutes. Drain well, pack in plastic freezer bags or boxes. Sharp freeze. To use, remove from freezer just before cooking. *Do not thaw*. Steaming is recommended.

Peppers: Wash and remove stem and seeds. Blanch in boiling water bath for 2 minutes after water returns to boiling. Drain, chill in ice water for 5 minutes. Drain well, pack in freezer boxes. Sharp freeze. To use, remove from freezer just before cooking. *Do not thaw.* Steaming is recommended.

Pumpkin and Winter Squash: These must be cooked and pureed before freezing. Cut up pumpkin or squash, removing stem and seeds. Place in pressure cooker with ¾ cup water and cook for 8 to 10 minutes at 15 pounds pressure, or place in deep roasting pan, add ½ cup water, cover, and bake at 375° for 1½ hours. Puree cooked vegetable to remove any strings, discarding the outer skin. Pack in plastic freezer bags or boxes, sharp freeze. To use, remove from freezer just before cooking. *Do not thaw.* Steaming is recommended.

Note: It is difficult to freeze summer squash without their becoming very mushy when thawed and cooked. Enjoy them fresh, but don't try to process them for later use.

Jam and Jelly

Jam and jelly are usually made by adding pectin to fresh fruit, then adding refined sugar and lemon juice to make the pectin form a gel. Preserves are whole fruits, cooked until thick, with sugar added for flavor and additional thickening. Preserves can easily be made without adding refined sugar: concentrated fruit juices are used for both sweetening and liquid required, and the mixture is then cooked down to the right consistency. If gelatin is added, you don't have to cook down as much to thicken. Agar-agar can be used instead of gelatin for this purpose (one-half stick = one envelope plain gelatin). Preserves are stored in the refrigerator, which also helps keep them thick.

Jam, jelly, or preserves made without refined sugar will be much less sweet than those containing many cups of sugar. (All jelly sold in inter-state commerce contains not less than forty-five percent fruit and fifty-five percent sugar! Jam contains sixty-five to sixty-eight percent fruit, according to legal definitions.) Yours will taste like fruit—not like candy. I think this is a good change and hope you will agree after you have made a batch or two.

If you are going to make spreads without sugar, you also have some decisions to make about what to use for ingredients:

1. Which fruit(s) to use.
2. What form of sweetening to use: Fruit juice? Other sweet fruit? Date sugar? Honey?

3. Whether or not to use pectin. If so, regular pectin with glycerine added? Or special low methoxy pectin which only requires a small amount of calcium to jell? (More about these later.)
4. If not using pectin, which fruits to include to be sure there is enough natural pectin to make a satisfactory jell?

If you plan to use pectin, skip the next few pages and go directly to the recipe sections. This is the easy way—forget about how much pectin nature put into fruit and just use commercial pectin (regular or special) with results you can count on. Nobody will know the difference in the end—and you'll have better results while saving a lot of time and testing.

Where do you start? Let's begin by looking at Table 3 on page 50 which shows how much natural pectin and acid fruits contain.

Note that tart fruit has more pectin than ripe, sweet fruit. This means that adding a small amount of tart fruit will greatly increase the natural pectin of the mixture. For example, use tart apples with apricots, perhaps only one-fourth to three-fourths volume. Or combine raspberries and strawberries with a very small amount of tart apple for good pectin content.

For fruits low in acid, add lemon juice or combine with one of the high acid fruits. For example: strawberries are low in pectin but adequate in acid; combine them with tart apples which are the reverse and you get a balanced combination. (Add some lemon juice and use ripe berries for sweetness.)

High heat destroys the natural pectin in fruit. Simmer the fruit—don't keep it boiling or you will not get a satisfactory jell.

How to check pectin in fruit combinations

First, put together combinations you think you will like, adjusting amounts until they taste good. It's not important if the fruits have enough pectin. You can add that. What is important is that you like the taste and texture of the mixture. Then add your choice of concentrated fruit juice, enough to make it sweet to your taste. Now check to see what amount of pectin is present. Directions for two ways to do this follow:

Method #1: Remove one cup mixture and place in separate saucepan. Add one-half tablespoon glycerine. Stir to mix, then return to heat and bring to rolling boil for one minute. Remove from heat and pour into dish to cool. (You may hurry the cooling by placing in freezer once it has cooled a little.) Check to see if you have a firm jell. If not, you will need to add some kind of pectin. If you have a partial jell, add half the recommended amount of pectin (see next section). Return this mixture to the original pot, stir, then add pectin, etc. It won't hurt to reheat the

Table 3
Classification of Fruits According to
Pectin and Acid Content

Adequate Pectin and Acid

Apples, tart	Limes
Blackberries, sour	Loganberries
Cherries, sour	Oranges, sour
Cranberries	Plums, Damson
Currants	and other sour
Gooseberries	varieties
Grapefruit	Quinces, tart
Grapes, American	Raspberries, red
Guavas, sour	and black
Lemons	

Adequate Pectin, Low Acid

Bananas, unripe	Melon, ripe
Cherries, sweet	Quinces, ripe
Figs, unripe	

Low Pectin, Adequate Acid

Apricots	Strawberries,
Rhubarb	most varieties

Low Pectin, Low Acid

Figs, ripe	Pears, ripe
Peaches, ripe	Bartlett
	Pomegranates

Source: Ruth M. Griswold. *The Experimental Study of Foods*. Boston: Houghton Mifflin Co., 1962.

glycerine but it will not jell again. Check the fruit's pectin before you make a batch and are unhappy with the result. If the mix contains at least half apple, that may be enough to jell the whole mixture, but don't count on it—check each batch of fruit.

Method # 2: This is a simpler method, but it involves throwing away your test sample. Stir together equal amounts fruit mixture and methyl alcohol (can be purchased from the drugstore but you have to sign the poison register, as it is toxic when swallowed). Let this mixture stand for five minutes and see what sort of jell you get. If only slightly thickened, add the entire amount of pectin called for in the recipe. If there is a nice thick jell, you don't have to add pectin, but without the alcohol you will have to add glycerine to get it to form a jell unless you are using honey. If there is enough honey in the mixture, it will cause jelling, just like sugar. Remember, *throw away the sample* and be sure to label the alcohol bottle as poison and store in a safe place.

More about Pectin

Pectin is a natural carbohydrate found in fruit, but the amount varies greatly between varieties and stages of ripeness (tart fruit is higher in natural pectin than ripe fruit). This natural jelling agent is what thickens jellies and jams. Apples are high-pectin fruits. Commercial pectin is generally made from apple pomace (residue left after juice is extracted) or from the white inner skin of citrus fruits. Apple pectin tends to make a more elastic jelly than that made from citrus fruit; however, most grocery store pectin comes from citrus fruit.

Acid must be added to make pectin jell unless the fruit itself has enough. Most jam and jelly recipes call for lemon juice, but other sources of acid could be vinegar, lime juice, citric acid, or tartaric acid. These give slightly different finished tastes compared to lemon juice. Since lemon juice works well in all recipes, that is what I recommend using unless you want to experiment with the others listed.

Earlier I mentioned that there are two types of pectin: regular (high methoxy pectin) and special (low methoxy pectin). The latter comes from citrus fruit and is chemically quite different from the grocery store pectin in that it uses a calcium solution, rather than sugar, to make a jell. Regular pectin is usually made to form a jell with sugar, but it also can be jelled using alcohol or glycerine. I recommend glycerine because it has no taste and the resulting texture is good. It is not digestible in the body and is totally harmless in the amounts suggested in our jam recipes. (USP grade glycerine [drugstore] is recommended. If no glycerine is used, these sugarless jams will not thicken properly.)

One pectin isn't any better—or worse—than the other; the structures vary and what it takes to make a jell varies accordingly. (If you don't want to add anything processed to your jam, use the preserve recipes. They are made by cooking down fruit and juices only; nothing is added to thicken, but the calorie count will be much higher and you won't get as much volume from the fruit. Since fruit is the most expensive item in your jam, getting less volume will make the cost higher per jar.) An advantage of special low methoxy pectin is that you can take pure fruit juice, add a little lemon for enhanced flavor, add the pectin solution and enough calcium to make it gel, and the result is beautiful jelly every time. Unfortunately, regular pectin does not make juice into good jelly without sugar.

This special pectin, often labeled "no sugar" pectin, is available in some health food stores and food cooperatives or by mail from Walnut Acres, Penns Creek, PA 17862. A package of the calcium needed to form the jell should be included with the pectin so you don't have to hunt for it (furnished as dicalcium phosphate). It, too, is a naturally occurring substance. One recipe takes very little calcium; the solution can be made up and kept refrigerated for several weeks. This pectin is more economical to use when making large batches of jam or jelly. Depending on shipping charges, the initial cost may be seven or eight dollars, but compared to sixty cents or more for each pectin package, it ends up cheaper. Send for it a few weeks early so you can study the directions ahead of time. It suggests Euell Gibbons's method for making sugarless jelly using boiling water in a blender to completely dissolve the pectin. This can then be refrigerated until needed. Dissolve the calcium ahead of time too, so the only time required is for gathering materials and heating juice. Recipes using this pectin as well as the regular pectin (with glycerine replacing sugar for thickening) are included in this book.

Using white grape juice to dissolve the pectin works wonderfully. It does not dilute the fruit, but flavors and sweetens it. Apple juice is good, too. Bring either to the boiling point, place in blender jar, and add pectin (one tablespoon per cup of hot juice). Blend for about one minute until completely dissolved. Pour into a container and cool; refrigerate until needed. That's all there is to it. The calcium solution is equally simple to make. In a container with a tight lid, place one cup water and one teaspoon of calcium powder. Shake to dissolve partially and place in refrigerator until needed. Shake each time before using as it does not completely dissolve and will have settled out.

Important: Commercial pectin powder lists dextrose as its first ingredient. This is sugar! Use liquid pectin (Certo) which does not contain any sugar. Add three ounces liquid pectin (one pouch) to four cups fruit or juice. And remember, without sugar use glycerine to get a jell. Directions are given with individual recipes.

Directions for Preparing Low Methoxy Pectin Solution

Heat white grape juice or apple juice* to boiling. If you wish to make a large batch of jelly, use four cups juice. Otherwise, use two cups juice plus four tablespoons water. Place this in the blender jar and add two and one-half tablespoons low methoxy pectin. Blend first on low and then on high for about one minute until all is in solution. Pour this into a wide-mouth jar or other container you can cover tightly. It will be thickening fast, so use a rubber spatula to remove it from the blender jar without wasting any. Work quickly when doing this and it will be much easier than if it has set up firm. This solution is used in the following recipes. Keep it refrigerated in a tightly covered jar until needed. It will melt in the hot jelly or jam.

* Concentrate apple juice slightly to make sugar content equal to that of the grape juice. For each cup juice needed, place one and one-third cups apple juice in saucepan and simmer to reduce volume to 1 cup (about ten to fifteen minutes on low heat).

Calcium Solution

Dissolve one teaspoon dicalcium phosphate in one cup water. This is best done in a jar, as you won't have to transfer it later. Screw the lid on the jar and put it in the refrigerator. Be sure to shake it well before pouring. It doesn't really dissolve, so much will settle out and have to be remixed each time.

If you have fairly soft water, you will need the amount of calcium suggested in these recipes. If your water is hard, you can use less because there is some calcium in your water—provided water is called for in that recipe. (The way to know if water is hard or soft is by how much soap you have to use to get suds—not much in soft water.)

How to Prepare Juice for Jelly

Juice for jelly is obtained by cooking the fruit until very soft, putting it into a jelly bag (purchase or make from several layers of cheesecloth), and allowing the liquid to drip into a container. This contains more pectin than the fruit juice you buy at the store. (Pectin comes from the skin and pulp, rather than just the juice.)

Fruit should be washed thoroughly to remove dirt or foreign material. Remove stems and blossom ends but leave skin and seeds. Chop into pieces and place in deep nonaluminum kettle, adding one-fourth cup water per cup of fruit (less if fruit is very juicy). Cover and simmer until fruit is very soft and juice has been extracted. (Using a masher to crush partly cooked fruit will speed up this process.) This will take from ten minutes to over half an hour.

Use jelly bag or make bag by folding several layers of wet cheesecloth within colander, being sure they drape over its edge each way so only juice can get through. Dampen bag or cheesecloth before pouring fruit into it. Suspend bag from hook or place colander over large bowl so juice can drip without remaining in contact with cooked fruit. Don't squeeze bag or jelly will be cloudy from suspended fruit particles. It will take several hours for all juice to drip out. (Check juice for pectin content by mixing with alcohol as described in the section on types of pectin. Add the total amount of pectin recommended if there is little; add half or less if pectin content is high.)

Jelly is usually made in small to medium batches: four to eight cups is best to work with. Glycerine-thickened and low methoxy pectins form after cooling down. You will have to trust your recipe, as you can't use any test to check at the final point.

What to Do if Jam or Jelly Doesn't Jell

Don't give up if your jelly doesn't jell or your jam isn't very thick. As mentioned earlier, there is a lot of difference between fruits—even the same tree from year to year will yield fruit which varies in pectin and acid content. That is why a trial batch should be made each time you start to process fruit. Thin jam or jelly is usually due to pectin which has not jelled, because of too much or too little acid, or lack of enough other material which causes jelling (glycerine or calcium solution). It isn't practical to redo the whole process—the fruit will be overcooked and mushy. The easy way is to add gelatin. Empty jelly or jam into kettle. Heat to boiling, sprinkle gelatin over hot mixture, mixing well to be sure it all dissolves. Since gelatin has no taste, you don't have to do anything to cover it up, although you can add a little lemon juice if you wish to sharpen the taste. One envelope of gelatin (one tablespoon) thickens four cups of quite runny jam or jelly. If less thickening is needed, reduce amount of gelatin. Fill clean, boiling-hot jars with jam or jelly and top with hot lids. If you have only a small amount, don't reprocess. Just refrigerate and eat soon. For larger amounts, process in boiling water bath ten minutes after water returns to boiling, or in pressure cooker ten minutes at five pounds pressure.

What to Use for Sweetening

Concentrated fruit juices are available frozen (grocery stores) and canned (health food stores, chiefly), and can be used undiluted to sweeten your preserves or as some or all of the liquid in jellies and jams. Concentrate juice yourself by simmering until reduced to half in volume. (Keep the heat very low while simmering to avoid an undesirable change in flavor.) There is much more sugar in concentrated juices than in the same juices when diluted. Because of this, they make good choices for use in canning and preserving. Fortunately, they are cheap and readily available.

As indicated in Table 4, a huge volume of juice is needed to get much sugar—the most concentrated available only contains approximately one-third cup sugar in one cup liquid juice. Naturally sweet fruit can be added to increase sweetness. Dried fruits are sweeter than fresh, because the drying process converts some of the sugars to forms that taste sweeter. For example, dried apples will have more sweetening effect than fresh. Dried apples, apricots, dates, pears, prune-plums—all need only be chopped or ground, then softened in liquid and added to fresh fruit.

Another good sweetening source is applesauce made with very sweet apples. It can be made quite thick (follow directions given in section on Canning but reduce liquid to one-half cup per quart chopped fruit) and pureed so that it is very smooth. It can be added to any other fruit without changing the flavor of the other fruit, provided you use one-third total volume applesauce or less (one-third cup this applesauce equals six teaspoons sugar).

Dried dates are another possible source of sweetening; date sugar is ground, dehydrated dates. This is very sweet, almost too sweet, and it has a distinct taste which can be unpleasant in certain combinations. Use it sparingly to give just a little boost in taste—and add some lemon juice along with it to help mask the date flavor: start with one teaspoon lemon juice for one-fourth cup date sugar, increasing lemon juice as you taste.

Table 4
Natural Sugar Content of Fruit Juices

Apple Juice
Regular juice equals 6 teaspoons per cup Concentrated juice equals 24 teaspoons per cup
White Grape Juice
Regular juice equals 8 teaspoons per cup Concentrated juice equals 16 teaspoons or more per cup   (simmered down to half volume)
Orange Juice
Regular juice equals 4 teaspoons per cup Frozen concentrate equals 16 teaspoons per cup
Pineapple Juice
Regular juice equals 6 teaspoons per cup Frozen concentrate equals 24 teaspoons per cup

Note: All sugars are not equally sweet, so these may not taste as sweet as their sugar content might lead you to expect.

Trial Batch

You cannot be sure, from year to year, that fruit will be sweet enough to suit you. Thus, it is important that you make a trial batch after deciding what combination(s) of fruit to try, which pectins to use (none for preserves), and what juice to use for sweetening. (This recipe does not use pectin and will not thicken; however, it does give you a chance to try the combination(s) before committing yourself to a whole batch.)

Trial Batch Recipe for Jam

Fruit 2½ cups peeled, pitted, and chopped
Concentrated fruit juice (plain juice or water) ¼ to ¾ cup
Lemon juice 2 teaspoons

Combine ingredients in small saucepan. Cover, simmer 5 to 8 minutes until fruit is soft (add a small amount of water if necessary). Remove from heat. Cool, taste, adjust sweetening. Makes 2 cups.
Note: This recipe represents the equivalent of light syrup. If not sweet enough, add date sugar or more concentrated fruit juice. Doubling the juice will make the equivalent of medium syrup.

Here is a list of combinations I have tried and liked well enough to remake. If you don't want to experiment, go right to the recipes which follow and you won't have to make any decisions about what to use or which to combine—it's all been done for you.

Table 5
Favorite Fruit Combinations

Apple and Apricot (½ and ½)
Apple and Cranberry (½ and ½)
Apple and Purple Grape Pulp (⅓ and ⅔) (no seeds and skins)
Apple and Quince (⅓ and ⅔)
Apple and Raspberry (⅓ and ⅔)
Apple and Strawberry (⅓ and ⅔)
Orange, Grapefruit, and Green Grapes (⅓ each)
Peach and Lemon (⅞ and ⅛) (grind lemon coarsely)
Peach, Pear and Apple (⅓ each) (plus cinnamon)
Pear and Lemon (⅞ and ⅛) (grind lemon coarsely)
Plum and Apple (¾ and ¼, or ½ and ½)
Raspberry and Strawberry (⅓ and ⅔, or ½ and ½)

Add lemon juice to all combinations (except those already containing lemon) to help bring out natural sweetness. Don't be afraid to try other mixtures. Some of my best jams came from odds and ends I threw together and then couldn't duplicate because I hadn't kept track of what went into the pot. (They surely were good while they lasted!)

Strawberry-Raspberry Jam

Very ripe berries   10 cups, stems removed
Concentrated apple juice   1 cup
Lemon juice   2½ tablespoons
Liquid pectin (regular)   6 ounces (1 package)
Glycerine   5 tablespoons
Salt   dash (optional)
Unflavored gelatin   1 to 2 tablespoons (1 to 2 envelopes) dissolved in
    ¼ cup boiling water

Place berries and fruit juices in deep kettle. Simmer until berries are tender, 10 to 12 minutes. (Mash the berries if you prefer the texture more uniform.) Remove from heat and stir in pectin, glycerine, and salt. Return to heat and bring to rolling boil. Boil exactly 1 minute. Remove from heat. Stir in gelatin (use 2 envelopes if berries are quite watery). Pour into hot, clean ½-pint jars, leaving ¾ inch at top. Cover with hot lids, screwed down tightly. Process in boiling water bath for 10 minutes after water has returned to boiling, or in pressure cooker for 10 minutes at 5 pounds pressure. Makes 10 cups.
* This jam can be made with any variety of berries, or with mixtures. If they are tart, add 2 or more tablespoons date sugar. Be sure to add at least 1 tablespoon more lemon juice if you use the date sugar. *Diabetics should not add this date sugar.*

Nutritional value: 2 tablespoons contain 12 Calories (P0,F0,C3). 6½ tablespoons equal 1 diabetic fruit exchange. If no salt is used, 3 tablespoons contain less than 1 milligram sodium.

Recipes Using Low Methoxy Pectin

Apricot-Pineapple Jam

Dried apricots   12-ounce package
Crushed pineapple   1¼ cups (in own juice)
Water   1½ cups (approximate)
Lemon juice   2 tablespoons
Concentrated orange juice (frozen, undiluted)   3 tablespoons
Lemon rind   1½ teaspoons grated
Salt   dash (optional)
Low methoxy pectin solution   ½ cup
Calcium solution   2½ teaspoons

Place apricots and pineapple in deep saucepan. Add enough water to completely cover fruit (about 1½ cups). Heat to boiling, cover, and set aside for 1 hour or longer to allow apricots to soften. Add lemon juice, orange juice, lemon rind, and salt, and reheat to boiling point. Add pectin solution, stir, return to heat, and return to boil. Remove from heat, add calcium solution, and mix well. Pour into hot, clean jars, leaving ¾ inch at top. Cap with hot lids. Place in boiling water bath for 10 minutes after water returns to boiling, or in pressure cooker for 10 minutes at 5 pounds pressure. Makes 6 cups.

Nutritional value: 1 tablespoon contains 12 Calories (P0,F0,C3). 3½ tablespoons equal 1 diabetic fruit exchange. If no salt is added, 1 tablespoon contains 1 milligram sodium.

Orange-Blueberry Jam

Blueberries, fresh or frozen whole   2 cups
Concentrated orange juice   ½ cup
Lemon juice   3 tablespoons
Orange or lemon rind   ½ teaspoon grated
Water   ½ cup
Low methoxy pectin solution   ¾ cup
Calcium solution   scant 4 teaspoons
Salt   dash (optional)

Place berries, juices, rind, and water in deep nonaluminum kettle. Bring to a boil, then turn down heat and cover. Simmer until fruit is done (about 10 minutes). (Leave lid slightly ajar or jam will run over.) Stir in special pectin solution. Return to heat and bring to a boil. Add calcium and salt, mix well. After removing from heat, skim and pack into hot, clean jars, leaving ¾ inch at top. Cap with hot lids. Process in boiling water bath for 10 minutes after water returns to boiling, or in pressure cooker for 10 minutes at 5 pounds pressure. Makes 4 cups.

Nutritional value: 2 tablespoons contain 12 Calories (P0,F0,C3). 7 tablespoons equal 1 diabetic fruit exchange. If no salt is added, 7 tablespoons contain less than 1 milligram sodium.

Making Jam, Jelly, and Preserves

This section includes recipes using regular pectin and special low methoxy pectin and is followed by a section on preserves using no added pectin. Low methoxy pectin is easy to use. With it you can correct any batch of jam or jelly that is too soft or too firm; it makes good clear jellies without sugar and never fails to jell! Send for some and try it yourself.

Basic Jam Recipe

Fruit   10 cups chopped, stems and pits removed
Lemon juice   3 to 5 tablespoons (the higher amount for sweeter fruit)
Concentrated fruit juice (white grape, apple, or orange)   ¾ cup
Salt   dash (optional)
Regular or low methoxy pectin

Wash, dry, and chop or grind fruit. (Large pieces are not used in jam, so be sure pieces are small.) Place fruit in large nonaluminum kettle; add juices and salt. Cook over low heat, stirring frequently to prevent sticking. As foam forms, skim off and discard. When fruit is soft, remove from heat. You are now ready to add pectin.

For regular pectin, add:

Liquid pectin   3 to 6 ounces (½ to 1 package) (depending upon the natural pectin in fruit)
Glycerine   5 to 7 tablespoons
Unflavored gelatin   1 tablespoon (1 envelope) (optional)

Stir in pectin and glycerine, return to heat, and bring to rolling boil. Boil for exactly 1 minute. Remove from heat. Sprinkle gelatin over hot mixture, stirring to completely dissolve. Pack into clean, hot jars, leaving ¾ inch at top. Cover with hot lids. Process in boiling water bath for 10 minutes after water has returned to boiling, or in pressure cooker for 10 minutes at 5 pounds pressure. Makes 11 cups using regular pectin.

For special, low methoxy pectin, add:

Low methoxy pectin solution   2 cups
Dicalcium phosphate solution   3 to 4 tablespoons (1 teaspoon per cup fruit)

Stir in pectin solution, then add calcium solution. Return to heat and bring to boil. Pack in clean, hot jars, top with hot lids, and process in boiling water bath for 10 minutes after water has returned to boiling, or in pressure cooker for 10 minutes at 5 pounds pressure.

Note: The jell sets up as it cools, so don't try to estimate firmness when it is hot. If it isn't firm enough when cooled, reheat and add more pectin and the corresponding amount of calcium solution. Put a small amount in a dish and chill in the freezer if you want to check the jell before you bottle the whole batch. Makes 12 cups using low methoxy pectin.

Nutritional value: Depending on fruit used, 1 tablespoon contains 4 to 12 Calories (P0,F0,C1-3)*. From 3½ to 10 tablespoons equals one diabetic fruit exchange. If no salt is added, 1 tablespoon contains less than 1 milligram sodium.
* These figures indicate grams of protein, fat, and carbohydrate per serving, and are given with each recipe. The food Calorie is the kilocalorie (1,000 calories) and is written with a capital "C" in this book.

Jam Recipes Using Regular Pectin

Apple-Berry Jam

Apples (pick sweet, soft apples like Yellow Transparents)   5 cups
   peeled, cored, and sliced
Strawberries, raspberries, or boysenberries   5 cups mashed or chopped
Concentrated apple juice   1 cup
White grape juice   1 cup
Liquid pectin (regular)*   3 to 6 ounces (½ to 1 package)
Glycerine   6 tablespoons
Salt   dash (optional)
Lemon juice   4 to 6 tablespoons (depending upon sweetness of apples)

Wash, dry, and prepare fruit. Place in large nonaluminum kettle. In separate pan combine apple and grape juices. Simmer to reduce volume to about 1 cup. Add to fruit, bring to boil, and simmer until fruit is soft, not more than 12 to 15 minutes. Remove from heat and mash to blend berries with apple pulp. Add pectin, glycerine, salt, and lemon juice. Return to heat after stirring to dissolve pectin. Bring to rolling boil. Boil exactly 1 minute. Remove from heat, pack immediately in hot, clean jars, leaving ¾ inch at top; cap with hot lids well screwed down. Process in boiling water bath for 10 minutes after water returns to boiling, or in pressure cooker 10 minutes at 5 pounds pressure. Store in cool, dark place to prevent color fading. Makes 12 cups.
* Unless you have checked the mixture's natural pectin content and know it is high, use the whole package (6 ounces) pectin.

Nutritional value: 1 tablespoon contains 12 Calories (P0,F0,C3). 3½ tablespoons equal 1 diabetic fruit exchange. If recipe is made without salt, 3 tablespoons contain 1 milligram sodium.

Apricot-Lemon Jam

Fresh apricots　9 cups quartered and pitted
Large lemon　½ sliced paper-thin
Lemon juice　4 tablespoons
Concentrated white grape juice　1 cup (simmered down from 2 cups)
Glycerine　6 tablespoons
Liquid pectin (regular)　6 ounces (1 package)
Salt　dash (optional)
Almond extract　¼ to ½ teaspoon
Unflavored gelatin　1 tablespoon (1 envelope), dissolved in some of the
　　grape juice

Pit and quarter apricots (leave a few pits in for flavor); slice lemon, removing seeds. Place fruit in large nonaluminum kettle, adding lemon juice and about half concentrated grape juice. Cook until tender, about 20 minutes. Remove from heat, add glycerine, pectin and salt, stirring well. Return to heat and boil for exactly 1 minute. Remove from heat, add almond extract plus gelatin dissolved in the remaining fruit juice (heated if necessary). Stir well. Pour into hot, clean jars, leaving ¾ inch at top, and cap with hot lids tightly screwed down. Process in boiling water bath for 10 minutes, or in pressure cooker 10 minutes at 5 pounds pressure. Store in cool, dark place. Makes 10½ cups.
Variation:　This can be made with dried apricots. Soak 24 ounces dried apricots in the 2 cups white grape juice. Allow to stand overnight to soften fruit. Drain liquid and simmer down to 1 cup. Follow recipe as directed.

Nutritional value:　1 tablespoon contains 5 Calories (P0,F0,C1¼). 8 tablespoons equal 1 diabetic fruit exchange. If no salt is added, 1 tablespoon contains less than 1 milligram sodium.

Apricot Marmalade

Fresh apricots   4 pounds or
>**Dried apricots**   1 pound, chopped and soaked
>>in the juice for 2 hours

Oranges   2, very thinly sliced
Lemon   ½, very thinly sliced
White grape juice   ¾ cup (simmered down from 1½ cups)
Concentrated orange juice   1 cup
Lemon juice   2 tablespoons
Liquid pectin (regular)   6 ounces (1 package)
Glycerine   6 tablespoons
Salt   dash (optional)
Unflavored gelatin*   1 tablespoon (1 envelope) (optional)

Remove pits from apricots and chop into ¼-inch pieces. Slice oranges
and lemons and remove seeds. Place fruit in large nonaluminum kettle.
Add grape juice and orange juice concentrate. Bring to a boil, then turn
down heat and simmer, covered, for about 15 minutes until fruit is soft.
Remove from heat. Add lemon juice, pectin, glycerine and salt. Stir.
Return to heat and bring to a boil, boiling for exactly 1 minute. Remove
from heat. Place in hot, clean jars, leaving ¾ inch at top. Cap with hot lids
firmly screwed down. Process in boiling water bath for 10 minutes after
water returns to boiling, or in pressure cooker for 10 minutes at 5 pounds
pressure. Makes 10 cups.
* If the hot marmalade is too thin, thicken it by adding gelatin just before
putting marmalade into jars. Sprinkle gelatin over hot fruit, stir well.

Nutritional value: 1 tablespoon contains 14 Calories (P0,F0,C3½). 3 tablespoons equal 1
diabetic fruit exchange. If made with no added salt, 3 tablespoons contain 3 milligrams
sodium.

Mixed Soft Fruit Jam

Apricots, peaches, pears, nectarines, etc.   10 cups sliced, finely chopped,
   or ground
Concentrated apple juice   ½ cup or
   Concentrated white grape juice   ⅔ cup (simmered
      down from 1⅓ cups)
Lemon juice   6 tablespoons
Whole cloves   1 tablespoon (optional)
Liquid pectin (regular)   6 ounces (1 package)
Glycerine   6 tablespoons
Salt   dash (optional)
Unflavored gelatin   1 tablespoon (1 envelope)

Peel and prepare fruit (leave a few pits in for almond flavor). Save juice
and put it and fruit in a deep nonaluminum kettle. Add fruit juice and
cloves and cook over low heat, stirring often. After fruit has come to a boil,
cover and cook until soft, 15 to 20 minutes at most. Remove from heat and
add pectin, glycerine, and salt. Stir well. Return to heat, bring to rolling
boil, and cook for exactly 1 minute. Remove from heat, pack in hot, clean
jars, leaving ¾ inch at top. Cap with hot lids firmly screwed down.
Process in boiling water bath for 10 minutes after water returns to boiling,
or in pressure cooker for 10 minutes at 5 pounds pressure. Makes 11
cups.
* If the hot jam seems a little too runny, make it thicker by adding 1
envelope of gelatin just before you put the marmalade into jars. Sprinkle
gelatin over hot fruit, stirring well to completely dissolve.

Nutritional value: 1 tablespoon contains 10 Calories (P0,F0,C2½). 4 tablespoons equal 1
diabetic fruit exchange. If made with no added salt, 4 tablespoons contain less than 2
milligrams sodium.

Plum Jam

Ripe sweet plums 10 cups stemmed, pitted, and quartered
Concentrated white grape juice 1 cup (simmered down from 2 cups)
Lemon juice 6 tablespoons
Lemon rind 1½ tablespoons coarsely grated
Date sugar 6 tablespoons (use if plums are less sweet) (optional)
Liquid pectin (regular) 6 ounces (1 package)
Glycerine 6 tablespoons
Salt dash (optional)
Unflavored gelatin 1 tablespoon (1 envelope)* (optional)

Prepare fruit and place in large nonaluminum kettle. Add juices and rind.
Bring to a boil and simmer, covered, over low heat until fruit is soft—
about 12 to 15 minutes. Taste, add date sugar if desired, and stir well.
Remove from heat, add pectin, glycerine, and salt, stirring to mix. Return
to heat, bring to rolling boil, and boil exactly 1 minute. Remove from heat.
Place in hot, clean jars, leaving ¾ inch at top. Cap with hot lids, firmly
screwed down. Process in boiling water bath for 10 minutes after the
water returns to boiling, or in pressure cooker 10 minutes at 5 pounds
pressure. Makes 11 cups.
* If hot jam is too thin, thicken by adding 1 envelope unflavored gelatin
just before packing into jars. Sprinkle gelatin over hot fruit, stir well.
Note: To make preserves, cook longer to thicken and omit pectin and
glycerine.

Nutritional value: 3½ tablespoons contain 40 Calories (P0,F0,C10). 3½ tablespoons equal
1 diabetic fruit exchange. If no salt is used, 3 tablespoons contain less than 2 milligrams
sodium.

Strawberry Jam

Strawberries   2 cups stemmed and washed
Concentrated apple juice   ½ cup
Lemon juice   1½ tablespoons
Low methoxy pectin solution   ½ cup*
Calcium solution*   2½ teaspoons

Place berries and juices in deep kettle. Simmer until berries are soft, about 10 minutes. (Mash berries for thicker jam.) Add pectin solution and return to heat until completely dissolved. Remove from heat, stir in calcium solution, and pour into hot, clean jars, leaving ¾ inch at top. Cap with hot lids. Process in boiling water bath for 10 minutes after water returns to boiling, or in pressure cooker for 10 minutes at 5 pounds pressure. Makes 3 cups.
* If your water is quite soft, allow ¼ teaspoon more calcium solution.
Variation: To make strawberry sauce (for pancakes, etc.), use only ¼ cup special pectin solution and 1¼ teaspoons calcium solution. This will lower the Calories to 8 per 2 tablespoons; 10 tablespoons equal 1 diabetic fruit exchange.

Nutritional value: 2 tablespoons contain 12 Calories (P0,F0,C3). 6½ tablespoons equal 1 diabetic fruit exchange. If no added salt is used, 4 tablespoons contain 1 milligram sodium.

Basic Jelly

Concentrated fruit juice   2 cups (apple, orange, grape—simmered down from 5 cups)
Water   1 cup
Lemon juice   1 to 2 tablespoons
Low methoxy pectin solution   ¾ cup
Calcium solution   scant 4 teaspoons
Orange or lemon rind   ½ to 1 teaspoon grated (optional)
Salt   dash (optional)

Place juices and water in saucepan, add special pectin solution, and bring to boil. Stir in calcium solution, rind, and salt. Pour into hot, clean jars, leaving ¾ inch at top. Cap with hot lids. Process in boiling water bath for 10 minutes after water returns to boiling, or in pressure cooker for 10 minutes at 5 pounds pressure. Makes 4 cups.

Nutritional value: 1 tablespoon contains 8 to 12 Calories (P0,F0,C2-3). 3½ to 5 tablespoons equal 1 diabetic fruit exchange. If no salt is added, 5 tablespoons contain less than 1 milligram sodium.

Apple Jelly

Concentrated apple juice (frozen, undiluted) 2½ cups
Water 1½ cups
Lemon juice 1½ tablespoons
Low methoxy pectin solution 1 cup
Calcium solution 5 teaspoons
Salt dash (optional)

Place juices and water in deep saucepan. Heat to boiling. Add pectin solution, reheat until completely dissolved; bring to full boil. Remove from heat, add calcium solution and salt. Stir well. Immediately pour into clean, hot jars; top with hot lids. Process in boiling water bath for 10 minutes after water returns to boiling, or in pressure cooker 10 minutes at 5 pounds pressure. If any jars fail to seal, refrigerate and use within 10 days. Makes 5 cups.

Note: Use this base for flavored jellies such as geranium, mint, and herb mixtures. Steep geranium or other leaves with hot apple juice, having first crushed them to release volatile odors and flavor. Strain out leaves/herbs, and continue with recipe as directed. Add ¼ teaspoon coloring if desired: (red for geranium, green for mint, etc.).

Nutritional value: 1 tablespoon contains 12 Calories (P0,F0,C3). 3½ tablespoons equal 1 diabetic fruit exchange. If made without salt, 3½ tablespoons contain less than 1 milligram sodium.

Orange Juice Jelly

Concentrated orange juice (frozen, undiluted)   1 cup
Water (or white grape juice for sweeter jelly)   1 cup
Orange rind   1 teaspoon grated
Lemon juice   1 tablespoon
Low methoxy pectin solution   ½ cup
Salt   dash (optional)
Calcium solution   2 to 2½ teaspoons

Mix juices and rind in deep saucepan. Heat to boiling, add pectin solution and salt, and bring to full boil. Remove from heat and add calcium solution. Stir well. Pour into hot, clean jars, leaving ¾ inch at top. Cap with hot lids. Process in boiling water bath for 10 minutes after water returns to boiling, or in pressure cooker for 10 minutes at 5 pounds pressure. Makes 2½ cups.

Variation: Substitute another concentrated juice in place of orange: try frozen concentrated pineapple juice and substitute lemon rind for orange.

Nutritional value: 1 tablespoon contains 12 Calories (P0,F0,C3). 3½ tablespoons equal 1 diabetic fruit exchange. With pineapple juice, 1 tablespoon contains 16 Calories (P0,F0,C4). 2½ tablespoons equal 1 diabetic fruit exchange. If made without salt, 4 tablespoons contain 1 milligram sodium.

Preserves

Most fruits can be used to make preserves, but expensive fruits will go further with some apple included. Up to one-third of the total volume can be apple and it will still taste and look undiluted. Unless the fruit is very sweet, or dried fruit is added, you will probably want to add sweetening. Concentrated fruit juices work well, with date sugar added to give needed zip in a few combinations. (Add date last, if at all.)

You may want to make fruit go further by thickening with gelatin or agar-agar and not cooking down as much. (Use one envelope gelatin as directed in jam recipes or dissolve one-half stick of agar-agar in one-half cup water, breaking into small pieces and allowing to soak. When almost dissolved, heat to finish melting. This will remain firm at room temperature, while gelatin has to be kept chilled to stay thick.)

Preserves freeze beautifully and will not "water" when thawed. To freeze, simply allow to cool to room temperature after packed, then place in sharp freeze section of freezer. To use, thaw overnight in refrigerator.

Suggested Combinations for Preserves

Apricot and Apple with Lemon
Apple, Lemon, and Date
Plum, Apple, and Orange
Orange, Grapefruit, and Apple (use small amounts of orange rind,
    concentrated orange juice, and lemon)
Raspberry and Apple
Strawberry and Apple
Strawberry and Raspberry with Apple

This only begins to suggest fruits you can combine. Most fruits blend together and if you try a Trial Batch as suggested, you can adjust the amounts of each to find which you like best.

Basic Preserve Recipe

Fruit or berries   7½ cups washed, pitted, chopped
Apples   2½ cups peeled, cored, sliced
Concentrated apple juice   1 cup or
    White grape juice   1 cup (simmered down from 2 cups)
Lemon juice   ¼ cup plus 2 teaspoons
Finely minced rind from ¼ medium lemon
Salt   dash (optional)
Unflavored gelatin   1 tablespoon (1 envelope) (optional) or
    Agar-Agar   ½ stick, dissolved in ½ cup water (optional)*
Spices (cinnamon, nutmeg, cloves, etc.)   1 teaspoon

Prepare fruit, place in large nonaluminum kettle. Stir in juices and rind. Simmer slowly over low heat until thickened, stirring frequently. (Fruit may be mashed for more uniform preserves.) Depending upon fruits selected, it may take 2 hours or more to thicken. Cooking should be interrupted when it is almost thick enough and salt, gelatin or agar-agar, and spices, if any, added. Remove from heat, skim, if necessary. Pour into hot, clean jars, topped with hot lids. Process in boiling water bath for 10 minutes after water has returned to boiling, or in pressure cooker for 10 minutes at 5 pounds pressure. To freeze, allow to reach room temperature, then place in sharp freeze section of freezer until hard. Remove to main freezer area for storage. To use, thaw overnight in refrigerator. Makes 7½ cups.
* If gelatin or agar-agar is used, preserves must be strained to ensure dissolving.

Nutritional value: 2 tablespoons contain 40 Calories (P0,F0,C10). 2 tablespoons equal 1 diabetic fruit exchange. If no salt is added, 2 tablespoons contains less than 3 milligrams sodium.

Apple Butter

Apples 6 cups peeled, diced
Concentrated apple juice 1½ cups
Apple cider 4½ cups
Lemon juice 7 tablespoons
Cinnamon 1 tablespoon
Nutmeg 1 teaspoon
Cloves ¾ to 1 teaspoon
Salt ⅛ teaspoon (optional)

Peel and core apples and remove stem and blossom ends. Place in large nonaluminum kettle, add apple juice, cider, and lemon juice. Cook over low heat until volume is reduced to about half (the consistency of applesauce). Stir frequently to avoid sticking. Add spices and salt, mix well. Heat 1 to 2 minutes to blend spice flavors with fruit. Remove from heat. Pack in hot, clean jars, leaving ¾ inch at top. Cap with hot lids, firmly screwed down. Process in boiling water bath 10 minutes after water returns to boiling. To freeze, allow to reach room temperature, then place in sharp freeze section of freezer until hard. Remove to main freezer for storage. Makes 6 cups.

Nutritional value: 1 tablespoon contains 16 Calories (P0,F0,C4). 2½ tablespoons equal 1 diabetic fruit exchange. If made without added salt, 2½ tablespoons contain less than 1 milligram sodium.

Cherry Conserve

Dark, sweet cherries   3 cups pitted and chopped
Concentrated apple juice   2 cups
Large orange   1 finely chopped, including ½ rind and juice
Lemon juice   2 tablespoons
Lemon rind   ½ to 1 teaspoon
Walnuts or pecans   ½ cup coarsely chopped
Salt   dash (optional)

Cook cherries with apple juice until slightly thickened. Add remaining ingredients. Cook until thickened, stirring often to prevent sticking. Pour into hot, clean ½-pint jars, leaving ¾ to 1 inch at top. Cap with hot jar lids, firmly screwed down. Process in boiling water bath for 10 minutes after water has returned to boiling, or process in pressure cooker 10 minutes at 5 pounds pressure. To freeze, cool to room temperature, then place in sharp freeze section of freezer until hard. Remove to main freezer for storage, or keep refrigerated and it will be good for 10 days or more. Makes 5½ cups.

Nutritional value: 1 tablespoon contains 16 Calories (P0,F0,C4). 2½ tablespoons equal 1 diabetic fruit exchange. If no salt is added, 4 tablespoons contain 1 milligram sodium.

Peach Butter

Very ripe peaches   2 quarts peeled, pitted, chopped
Apple cider   3 cups
Concentrated white grape juice   1 cup (simmered down from 2 cups)
Lemon juice   2 tablespoons
Lemon rind   ¼ to ½ teaspoon grated (to taste)
Salt   dash (optional)
Almond extract   ½ teaspoon (optional)

Place all ingredients (except almond extract) in large nonaluminum kettle. Cook over low heat until thick, stirring frequently and skimming if necessary. When suitably thick, taste. Add extract if desired. Pour into hot, clean jars, cap with hot lids firmly screwed down. Process in boiling water bath for 10 minutes after water has returned to boiling, or in pressure cooker for 10 minutes at 5 pounds pressure. To freeze, cool to room temperature, then place in sharp freeze section of freezer until hard. Remove to main freezer for storage, or keep refrigerated and it will be good 10 days or more. Makes 6 to 7 cups.

Nutritional value: 2 tablespoons contain 20 Calories (P0,F0,C5). 4 tablespoons equal 1 diabetic fruit exchange. If no salt is added, 4 tablespoons contain less than 1 milligram sodium.

Strawberry Date Nut Preserves

Fresh or frozen whole strawberries*   2 cups halved
Dates   ½ cup chopped medium-fine
White grape juice   1 cup (simmered down from 2 cups)
Lemon rind   1 teaspoon grated
Lemon juice   1½ tablespoons
Salt   dash (optional)
Walnuts or pecans   ½ cup chopped

Combine all ingredients except nuts in a deep saucepan. Simmer over low heat until fairly thick. Stir in nuts. Return to heat and continue to cook until thick, stirring frequently to prevent sticking. Remove from heat. Pour into hot, clean jars, leaving ¾ inch at top. Cover with hot lids firmly screwed down. Process in boiling water bath for 10 minutes after water returns to boiling, or in pressure cooker for 10 minutes at 5 pounds pressure. To freeze, cool to room temperature, then place in sharp freezing area of freezer until hard. Remove to main freezer for storage. Makes 2½ cups.
* These preserves can be made with other berries, but strawberries are best.

Nutritional value: 1 tablespoon contains 27 Calories (P0,F½,C4½). 2 tablespoons equal 1 diabetic fruit exchange. If no salt is added, 2 tablespoons contain less than 1 milligram sodium.

Freezing Jam

You can't make the usual freezer jam without adding large amounts of corn syrup (sugar!). Without this corn syrup, the water in the jam will form hard crystals and when frozen will be rock-hard. Honey can be substituted for the corn syrup in equal amounts and the resulting jam will not freeze hard, but the honey flavor will overpower the natural fruit taste.

No-sugar-added jam cannot be used directly from the freezer, but may be frozen to preserve it and thawed before being used. If you add gelatin (or agar-agar) for part of the thickening, it will remain firm when thawed. Just add the gelatin along with the pectin, being sure it dissolves completely. Try "Lazy Person's Jam," a simple recipe that does not use pectin but relies completely on gelatin for thickening. Also included is a basic frozen jam recipe that is very good and does not "water" badly when thawed. To use these frozen jams, thaw overnight in the refrigerator. Keep refrigerated and they will stay good for ten days or more. If you thaw them too fast (at room temperature), they will separate and be watery.

Making jelly for freezing, without adding sugar, requires gelatin or some form of pectin to keep it jelled after thawing. Special low methoxy pectin works best and some recipes using it have been included. Jelly thickened with gelatin or ordinary pectin tends to weep badly after being thawed more than two to three days. For firm jam or jelly, when you plan to freeze it until used, make the pectin content a little higher: add ¼ cup additional special pectin and 1¼ teaspoons additional calcium solution. (These frozen jam recipes include these extra amounts; don't increase the amount any more or it will be too stiff.)

Frozen Jam Recipes Using Regular Pectin

Basic Recipe

Fresh fruit   10 cups sliced or chopped, stems and pits removed
Concentrated apple juice   ½ cup or
  Concentrated white grape juice   ⅔ cup (simmered down from
    1⅓ cups)
Lemon juice   3 tablespoons
Lemon rind   ¼ to ½ teaspoon grated
Liquid pectin (regular)   6 ounces (1 package)
Glycerine   6 tablespoons
Salt   ⅛ teaspoon (optional)
Unflavored gelatin   2 tablespoons (2 envelopes)

Mash half the fruit, add juices, rind, pectin, glycerine, and salt. Bring to a hard boil and boil for 1 minute, stirring constantly. Remove from heat, add remainder of fruit (pieces or mashed). Add gelatin by sprinkling over hot mixture, stirring well to dissolve, or dissolve it in ¼ cup hot water before adding. Cool slightly; pack into small jars or containers, leaving ¾ inch for expansion when freezing. Cover tightly, place in sharp freeze section of freezer. When firm, remove to other shelf for storage. Makes 10½ cups.

Nutritional value: 1 tablespoon contains 6 Calories (P0,F0,C1½). This can be used in small amounts without diabetic replacement. 6 tablespoons equal 1 diabetic fruit exchange. If made without added salt, 1 tablespoon contains less than 1 milligram sodium.

Frozen Blueberry Jam

Blueberries   10 cups washed, stems removed
Concentrated apple juice   ½ cup or
    Concentrated white grape juice   ⅔ cup (simmered down from
       1⅓ cups) or
    Concentrated orange juice   ⅔ cup (frozen, undiluted)
Lemon juice   4 tablespoons
Lemon rind   ½ teaspoon grated
Salt   ½ teaspoon (optional)
Nutmeg   ½ teaspoon (optional)
Liquid pectin (regular)   6 ounces (1 package)
Glycerine   6 tablespoons
Gelatin   1 tablespoon (1 envelope) (optional)

Place fruit, juices, lemon rind, and salt in deep saucepan. Bring to a hard boil for 1 minute. Remove from heat and add nutmeg, pectin, and glycerine. Return to heat and bring to a rolling boil for 1 minute. Stir in gelatin by sprinkling over top of hot liquid and stirring well to dissolve. Pour into sterile jars, top with sterile lids. Set aside to cool to room temperature. When cool, place in sharp freeze portion of freezer. When hard, move to other shelf for storage. To use, thaw overnight in refrigerator. Makes 10 to 10½ cups.
* Gelatin is added to keep jam thicker after freezing. Without it, jam will be fairly thin when thawed more than a day or two.

Nutritional value: 1 tablespoon contains 8 Calories (P0,F0,C2). 5 tablespoons equal 1 diabetic fruit exchange. If made without added salt, 5 tablespoons contain less than 1 milligram sodium.

Frozen Boysenberry Jam

Boysenberries   10 cups washed and hulled
Lemon juice   3 tablespoons
Lemon rind   2 teaspoons grated
Liquid pectin (regular)   6 ounces (1 package)
Glycerine   5 tablespoons
Salt   dash (optional)
Concentrated apple juice   1 cup and
    White grape juice   ½ cup (simmered down to 1 cup total)
Unflavored gelatin   2 tablespoons (2 envelopes)
Cold water   ½ cup

Mash or crush half boysenberries and place in nonaluminum kettle; add lemon juice, rind, pectin, glycerine, fruit juices, and salt. Bring to a full rolling boil for exactly 1 minute, stirring constantly. Remove from heat; add remainder of berries (whole or crushed, as you prefer). Add gelatin to ½ cup cold water; allow to stand about 5 minutes, then warm to dissolve completely; add to berry mixture. Allow to cool slightly. Pour into jars or freezer containers, leaving ¾ inch for expansion. Keep frozen until ready for use. Thaw in refrigerator 24 hours before using. Use within 10 days of thawing to prevent spoiling. Makes 10½ cups.

Nutritional value: 1 tablespoon contains about 6 Calories (P0,F0,C1½). 7 tablespoons equal 1 diabetic fruit exchange. If made without salt, 7 tablespoons contain less than 1 milligram sodium.

Frozen Strawberry Jam

Strawberries   10 cups washed and hulled
Lemon juice   2 tablespoons
Liquid pectin (regular)   6 ounces (1 package)
Glycerine   5 tablespoons
Salt   dash (optional)
Concentrated white grape juice   1 cup (simmered down from 3 cups)
Unflavored gelatin   2 tablespoons (2 envelopes)
Cold water   ½ cup

Mash half berries after cleaning and culling any overripe or green; place in nonaluminum kettle with lemon juice, pectin, glycerine, salt, and grape juice. Bring to a full rolling boil for 1 minute, stirring constantly. Remove from heat. Add remainder of berries (diced, sliced, or whole). Combine gelatin with water; allow to stand 5 minutes; then heat gently to dissolve. Add to berries, stir well to mix. Allow to cool slightly before packing into jars. Pour into jars or freezer cartons. Cover. Place on coldest shelf in freezer to allow quick freezing. Store in freezer until use. Thaw for 24 hours in refrigerator before use. Use within 10 days of thawing. Makes 10½ cups.

Note: If fruit is not sweet and ripe, it will not make good jam, but be sure not to oversweeten. This jam tastes sweeter cold than warm and first cooked.

Nutritional value: 1 tablespoon contains 4 Calories (P0,F0,C1). 10 tablespoons equal 1 diabetic fruit exchange. 2 tablespoons of jam may be used without replacement. If made without adding salt, 10 tablespoons contain less than 1 milligram sodium.

Frozen Jam Recipes Using Low Methoxy Pectin

Basic Recipe

Fresh fruit   4 cups pitted and chopped
Concentrated apple juice   1 cup or
    White grape juice   1 cup (simmered down from 2 cups)
Lemon juice   4 tablespoons
Lemon rind   ½ teaspoon grated (add with lemon juice) (optional)
Low methoxy pectin solution   ¾ cup
Calcium solution   scant 4 teaspoons
Cinnamon   1 teaspoon (optional)
Nutmeg   ½ teaspoon (optional)
Salt   dash (optional)

Place fruit in deep nonaluminum kettle. Add juices and rind and simmer until very soft. Add pectin solution (and spices and salt if desired). Reheat to boiling, add calcium solution, skim, and pour immediately into hot, sterile jars, leaving ½ inch at top for expansion when freezing. Top with sterile lids and set aside to cool until room temperature. Place on freezing shelf in freezer until hard. Remove to other area of freezer for storage. To use, thaw overnight in refrigerator. Makes 5½ cups.

Nutritional value: 1 tablespoon contains 8 to 10 Calories (P0,F0,C2-2½), depending upon fruit used. 4 to 5 tablespoons equal 1 diabetic fruit exchange. If no salt is added, 2 tablespoons contain less than 1 milligram sodium.

Frozen Berry Jam

Berries (strawberries, raspberries, boysenberries)   4 cups washed and
    halved
Concentrated white grape juice   1 cup (simmered down from 2 cups)
Lemon juice   4 tablespoons
Lemon rind   ¼ teaspoon grated (optional)
Salt   dash (optional)
Low methoxy pectin solution   ¾ cup
Calcium solution   scant 4 teaspoons

Place berries, juices, rind, and salt in deep saucepan. Bring to a boil. Add pectin solution; reheat to boiling. Remove from heat, add calcium solution, and mix well. Pour into sterile jars and top with sterile lids. Set aside to cool. When cooled to room temperature, place in sharp freeze section of freezer, removing to other shelf for storage when hard. To use, thaw overnight in refrigerator. Makes 5½ cups.

Nutritional value: 2 tablespoons contain 12 Calories (P0,F0,C3). 7 tablespoons equal 1 diabetic fruit exchange. If no salt is added, 7 tablespoons contain less than 1 milligram sodium.

Frozen Blueberry-Orange Jam

Blueberries 4 cups washed, stems removed
Concentrated orange juice ½ cup
Lemon juice 4 tablespoons
Lemon rind ¼ to ½ teaspoon (optional)
Water ½ cup
Low methoxy pectin solution ¾ cup
Calcium solution scant 4 teaspoons
Nutmeg ¼ teaspoon (optional)
Salt dash (optional)

Place fruit in deep nonaluminum kettle. Add juices, rind, and water and simmer until fruit is very soft. Add pectin solution (and spices if desired). Reheat to boiling, add calcium solution, skim, and pour immediately into hot, sterile jars, leaving ½ inch at top for expansion. Top with sterile lids and set aside to cool until room temperature. Place on freezing shelf in freezer until hard. Remove to other shelf of freezer for storage. To use, thaw overnight in refrigerator. Makes 5½ cups.

Nutritional value: 1 tablespoon contains 8 Calories (P0,F0,C2). 5 tablespoons equal 1 diabetic fruit exchange. If no salt is added, 2 tablespoons contain less than 1 milligram sodium.

Frozen Raspberry Jam

Raspberries   4 cups, washed, stems removed
White grape juice   ½ cup (simmered down from 2 cups)
Lemon juice   4 tablespoons
Lemon rind   ¼ teaspoon grated (optional)
Low methoxy pectin solution   ¾ cup
Calcium solution   scant 4 teaspoons
Salt   dash (optional)

Place fruit in deep nonaluminum kettle. Add juices and rind, cover, and place over low heat. Simmer until fruit is soft (8 minutes). Add pectin and return to heat, bringing to a boil. Remove from heat, add calcium and salt. Mix well. Skim and pour immediately into hot sterile jars, leaving ¾ inch at top for expansion. Cover with sterile lids and cool to room temperature before freezing. When cool, place on sharp freeze shelf and leave until very hard. Move to other shelf for storage. To use, thaw overnight in refrigerator. Makes 5½ cups.

Nutritional value: 1 tablespoon contains 8 Calories (P0,F0,C2). 5 tablespoons equal 1 diabetic fruit exchange. If no salt is added, 2 tablespoons contain less than 1 milligram sodium.

Frozen Jam Recipes Using Gelatin or Agar-Agar

Basic Recipe
(Lazy Person's Jam)

Fresh fruit   4 cups washed and chopped
Concentrated white grape juice   1 cup (simmered down from 2 cups) or
    Concentrated apple juice   ⅔ cup
Lemon   ¼, chopped with juice or
    Lemon juice   2¼ tablespoons
Unflavored gelatin   2 tablespoons (2 envelopes) or
    Agar-agar   1 stick*
Salt   dash (optional)

Place chopped fruit, juice, and chopped lemon into a deep saucepan. Cover and simmer for 8 minutes until fruit is barely cooked. Remove from heat and sprinkle gelatin over hot mixture, stirring well to dissolve evenly. Add spices (see **Variations**) and salt, taste, and adjust seasoning. Pour into clean, hot jars with hot lids and set aside to cool to room temperature. Freeze in sharp freeze section of freezer, then remove to other shelf for storage. To use, thaw overnight in refrigerator. Makes 4½ to 5 cups.

* If using agar-agar, break into small pieces and soak in ½ cup warm water for approximately 1 hour. Gently heat to dissolve any solid pieces. Add as directed for gelatin.

Variations:

With apple: Add ½ teaspoon cinnamon + ¼ teaspoon nutmeg + ⅛ teaspoon ginger (or more of each if you like it spicy)

With berries: Add 1 tablespoon lemon juice extra

With plums: Add ¼ to ½ teaspoon nutmeg or ground cloves

With sour apples: Add ¼ cup chopped raisins (soak in hot juice before using juice with fruit)

Nutritional value: 1 tablespoon contains 4 to 8 Calories (P0,F0,C1-2), depending upon fruit used. 5 to 10 tablespoons equal 1 diabetic fruit exchange. If no salt is added, 5 tablespoons contain 1 milligram sodium.

Lazy Person's Peach Jam

Peaches 4 cups peeled, pitted and chopped
Lemon rind ¼ teaspoon grated
Lemon juice 2½ tablespoons
Concentrated white grape juice 1 cup (simmered down from 2 cups)
Unflavored gelatin 1½ tablespoons (1½ envelopes)
Cinnamon ½ teaspoon
Salt dash (optional)
Nutmeg ¼ teaspoon (optional)
Ginger ¼ teaspoon (optional)

Place chopped fruit, rind, and juices into a deep saucepan. Cover and simmer for 8 minutes until fruit is barely cooked. Remove from heat and sprinkle gelatin over hot mixture, stirring well to dissolve. Add spices and salt, taste, and adjust seasoning. Pour into clean, hot jars with hot lids and set aside to cool to room temperature. Freeze in sharp freeze section of freezer, then remove to main section for storage. To use, thaw overnight in refrigerator. Makes 5 cups.

Nutritional value: 1 tablespoon contains 8 Calories (P0,F0,C2). 5 tablespoons equal 1 diabetic fruit exchange. If no salt is added, 1 tablespoon contains less than 1 milligram sodium.

Lazy Person's Plum Jam

Dried prunes   4 cups pitted, soaked before measuring*
Prune juice   ½ cup
Lemon juice   3 tablespoons
Concentrated white grape juice   ½ cup (simmered down from 1 cup)
Water   ½ cup
Lemon rind   ½ teaspoon grated
Nutmeg   ½ teaspoon or
    Cloves   ¼ teaspoon
Salt   dash (optional)
Unflavored gelatin   1 tablespoon (1 envelope)

Soak prunes in juices and water overnight to soften. Place in deep nonaluminum saucepan and simmer until soft. Mash to break up pieces and return to heat. Add rind, spices, and salt and sprinkle gelatin over hot mixture, stirring well. Pour into sterile jars, leaving ¾ inch at top for expansion. Cover with sterile lids and cool to room temperature. Freeze in sharp section of freezer, removing to other section for storage. To use, thaw overnight in refrigerator. Makes 5 cups.
* Depending upon size of prunes, it will take from 1½ to 2 cups dried to make 4 cups after soaking.

Nutritional value: 1 tablespoon contains 10 Calories (P0,F0,C2½). 4 tablespoons equal 1 diabetic fruit exchange. If no salt is added, 1 tablespoon contains less than 1 milligram sodium.

Easy Frozen Berry Jam

Strawberries   4 cups halved
Concentrated white grape juice   ½ cup (simmered down from 1½ cups)
Lemon juice   2½ tablespoons
Lemon rind   ¼ teaspoon grated
Unflavored gelatin   1½ tablespoons (1½ envelopes)
Salt   dash (optional)

Place berries, juices, rind, and salt in saucepan. Mash berries to release juice. Heat to boiling, sprinkle gelatin over hot mixture, stirring well to dissolve. Remove from heat, skim, and pack immediately into hot, sterile jars, topped with sterile lids. Set aside to cool to room temperature. When cool, freeze in sharp freeze section of freezer; remove to main section for storage. To use, thaw overnight in refrigerator. Makes 4½ cups.

Nutritional value: 1 tablespoon contains 6 Calories (P0,F0,C1½). 7 tablespoons equal 1 diabetic fruit exchange. If no salt is added, 1 tablespoon contains less than 1 milligram sodium.

Frozen Jelly Using Low Methoxy Pectin

Basic Frozen Jelly

Unsweetened fruit juice 2 cups
White grape juice 1 cup
Lemon juice 3 tablespoons
Low methoxy pectin solution 1½ cups
Salt dash (optional)
Calcium solution 6½ teaspoons

Place all juices in deep nonaluminum pan. Bring to a boil, add pectin and salt, and reheat to boiling. Remove from heat, add calcium solution. Skim and pour into sterile jars, topped with sterile lids. Cool to room temperature. When cool, place in sharp freeze section of freezer, removing to other shelf for storage. To use, thaw overnight in refrigerator. Makes 5 cups.

Nutritional value: 1 tablespoon contains between 6 to 12 Calories depending upon juice selected (P0,F0,C1½-3). From 3½ to 6½ tablespoons can equal 1 diabetic fruit exchange. Unless salt is added, 1 tablespoon contains less than 1 milligram sodium.

Frozen Apple Jelly

Concentrated apple juice 1½ cups
Lemon juice ¼ cup
Water 1½ cups
Lemon rind ½ teaspoon grated
Low methoxy pectin solution 1½ cups
Salt dash (optional)
Calcium solution 6½ teaspoons

Place all juices in deep nonaluminum pan. Bring to a boil, add pectin and salt, and reheat to boiling. Remove from heat, add calcium solution. Skim and pour into sterile jars, topped with sterile lids. Cool to room temperature. When cool, place in sharp freeze section of freezer, removing to other shelf for storage. To use, thaw overnight in refrigerator. Makes 5 cups.

Nutritional value: 1 tablespoon contains 12 Calories (P0,F0,C3). 3½ tablespoons equal 1 diabetic fruit exchange. If no salt is added, 1 tablespoon contains less than 1 milligram sodium.

Frozen Grape Jelly

Unsweetened Concord grape juice   2 cups (simmered down from 3 cups)
Unsweetened white grape juice   1 cup
Lemon juice   3 tablespoons
Low methoxy pectin solution   1½ cups
Salt   dash (optional)
Calcium solution   6½ teaspoons

Place all juices in deep nonaluminum pan. Bring to a boil, add pectin and salt, reheat to boiling. Remove from heat, add calcium solution. Skim and pour into sterile jars, topped with sterile lids. Cool to room temperature. When cool, place in sharp freeze section of freezer, removing to other areas for storage when hard. To use, thaw overnight in refrigerator. Makes 5 cups.

Nutritional value: 1 tablespoon contains 6 Calories (P0,F0,C1½). 6½ tablespoons equal 1 diabetic fruit exchange. If no salt is added, ½ cup contains less than 1 milligram sodium.

Frozen Orange Jelly

Concentrated orange juice   2 cups (frozen, undiluted)
White grape juice   1½ cups
Lemon juice   2 tablespoons
Orange or lemon rind   1½ teaspoons grated
Low methoxy pectin solution   ¾ cup
Calcium solution   scant 4 teaspoons
Salt   dash (optional)

Place all juices and rind in deep nonaluminum saucepan. Bring to a boil. Add pectin and reheat to boiling. Skim and stir in calcium solution and salt. Pour into sterile jars, top with sterile lids, and set aside to cool to room temperature. Place in sharp freeze section of freezer until hard and move to other shelf for storage. To use, thaw overnight in refrigerator. Makes 5 cups.

Nutritional value: 1 tablespoon contains 10 Calories (P0,F0,C2½). 4 tablespoons equal 1 diabetic fruit exchange. If no salt is added, 4 tablespoons contain 1 milligram sodium.

Fruit Sauces

Elegant and easy fruit sauces can be made from fruit and concentrated fruit juices, or by using less pectin in fruit jams. Low methoxy pectin works so perfectly with these sauces; do try some. These all make excellent replacements for sugar-containing syrups on pancakes and waffles.

Fruit Juice Sauce

Concentrated fruit juice   1 cup
Water   1 cup, boiling
Lemon rind   ¼ teaspoon grated (optional)
Lemon juice   1 tablespoon (optional)
Honey   1 tablespoon (optional)
Low methoxy pectin solution   ¼ cup
Calcium solution   1¼ teaspoons

Combine fruit juice, water, lemon rind, and lemon juice in saucepan. Add pectin solution and bring to a boil. Add calcium solution and return to heat, again bringing to a boil. Taste and add honey, if desired, before removing from heat. Pour into sterile jars, cover with sterile lids, and cool to room temperature before freezing. (Or process in boiling water bath for 10 minutes after water returns to boiling, or in pressure cooker for 10 minutes at 5 pounds pressure.) Makes 2¼ cups.

Nutritional value: Orange Juice Sauce: ¼ cup contains 52 Calories (P0,F0,C13). 3 tablespoons equal 1 diabetic fruit exchange. ¼ cup contains less than 2 milligrams sodium. If made with honey, ¼ cup contains 64 Calories (P0,F0,C16). *If made with honey, this sauce should not be used by diabetics.*

Apple Juice Sauce: If made without honey, ¼ cup contains 52 Calories (P0,F0,C13). 3 tablespoons equal 1 diabetic fruit exchange. ¼ cup contains less than 4 milligrams sodium.

Grape Juice Sauce: Made from 3 cups grape juice simmered down to 2 cups, water omitted: ¼ cup contains 56 Calories (P0,F0,C14). 3 tablespoons equal 1 diabetic fruit exchange. ¼ cup contains less than 4 milligrams sodium.

Cooked Fruit Sauce

Follow recipes in section using low methoxy pectin: Apricot-Pineapple, Pineapple, or Strawberry Jam recipes are good (see Index). Reduce pectin to ¼ cup and reduce calcium solution to 1¼ teaspoons. To make Orange-Blueberry Jam into syrup, reduce pectin to ⅜ cup and calcium solution to a scant 2 teaspoons. Nutritional values will be unchanged from those given. Be sure to freeze or process canned sauces in boiling water bath or pressure cooker so they will not spoil.

Meatless Mincemeat

An early 1800s cookbook refers to the ingredients for mincemeat as "a good piece of lean beef, boiled the day before it is needed. Half a pound of raw suet, chopped fine may be added . . . mix with twice the quantity of fine juicy apples . . . then put in the fruit, next the sugar and spice and lastly the liquor (brandy)." Other early recipes call for suet only, omitting lean beef. These recipes go one step further and omit the suet as well—creating vegetarian mincemeat!

Commercial mincemeat is very high in sugar. Make your own without added sweetening or use modest amounts of honey; the results will be very good. You'll need a meat grinder (a food processor does not make the right size pieces), patience, and the time to put it all together. Mincemeat can be frozen without processing. Put it into a tightly covered container and sharp freeze, moving to another area in the freezer when hard. Thaw overnight in refrigerator before use.

Basic Sugarless Vegetarian Mincemeat

Apple pulp   3 cups coarsely ground (including some skins)
Large lemon   ½, coarsely ground, including peel
Medium orange   1, coarsely ground, including peel
Seedless raisins   1 cup coarsely ground
Whole seedless raisins   1 cup
Currants   1 cup
Cinnamon   2 teaspoons
Nutmeg   ¾ teaspoon
Cloves   ¾ teaspoon
Allspice   ¾ teaspoon (optional)
Salt   ½ teaspoon
Flour   2 tablespoons or
    Arrowroot flour   1 tablespoon
Date sugar   ¼ cup (optional)
Brandy   ⅓ cup or
    Rum flavoring   1½ teaspoons

Quarter and core apples, but do not peel. Grind in old-fashioned meat grinder (food processor makes them too fine), using medium-coarse blade. Remove seeds from lemon and orange, grind, and add to apples, using medium blade. Grind 1 cup raisins. Mix all ingredients (except brandy) in large bowl, stirring in spices and flour, then date sugar if desired. Add brandy or rum flavoring and mix again. Place in covered bowl or other container with tight lid; refrigerate at least 2 days to age. (This mincemeat improves with standing, so one week's aging is not too much.) Makes 1 quart (enough for 2 large pies).

Note: This recipe is vegetarian and calls for no refined sugar. Make at least a week ahead and allow to age before use. The brandy will cook off during baking so you can serve it without allowing for those calories. In fact, no one will guess this is sugarless.

Nutritional value: ¼ cup contains 116 Calories (P1,F0,C28). ¼ cup equals 3 diabetic fruit exchanges. If no salt is added, ¼ cup contains 7 milligrams sodium.

Green Tomato Mincemeat

Green tomatoes   4 cups, peeled and chopped or coarsely ground
Apples   4 cups, cored, seeded, and chopped (half unpeeled)
Seedless raisins   4 cups (2 cups coarsely ground)
Currants   2 cups
Date sugar   8 tablespoons
Medium lemon   ½, including peel, coarsely ground
Cinnamon   1 tablespoon
Nutmeg   1½ teaspoons
Cloves   ¾ teaspoon
Allspice   ½ teaspoon (optional)
Salt   1 teaspoon
Flour   3 tablespoons
Brandy   ½ cup or
     Rum flavoring   2 teaspoons

Grind ingredients as directed for Basic Mincemeat, combining in large bowl. Stir to mix evenly. Add remaining ingredients, mixing after each addition. Place in covered container and refrigerate at least overnight or several days if not needed immediately. This may be frozen for future use but is better fresh. Thaw overnight in refrigerator before using. Makes 15 cups.

Nutritional value: ¼ cup contains 62 Calories (P½,F0,C15). ¼ cup equals 1 diabetic bread exchange (or 1½ diabetic fruit exchanges). ¼ cup contains 5 milligrams sodium.

Pickles, Relishes, and Seasoning Sauces

Although pickles are traditionally thought of as sour, sweet pickles (and some not-so-sweet)—bread-and-butter pickles, sweet relish, catsup, chili, cocktail sauce, and many others—are all loaded with sugar. But they don't have to be; they can be made without any sugar at all if you don't mind a slightly less "sweet" pickle.

Grandmother probably packed her hot pickles into sterile jars, put on hot lids, and that was that. Today we think it wiser to process them in a boiling water bath or pressure cooker to make sure they are bacteria-free and can be stored indefinitely.

Pickles don't freeze well; they get soft and mushy. If canned, they stay firm and crisp. Relishes and sauces can be frozen, if freezer space is available and time is short, but they taste better to me when they've been processed.

Bread-and-Butter Pickles

Cucumbers 9 large or 12 medium
Onions 2 small or 8 pickling size
Coarse pickling salt ¼ cup
White grape juice 3 cups (simmered down from 6 cups)
Vinegar (pickling strength) 1⅓ cups
Whole mustard seed ⅔ teaspoon
Celery seed ½ teaspoon
Black pepper 1 teaspoon
Turmeric powder scant ½ teaspoon

Score cucumbers lengthwise with tines of fork. Cut into medium-thick slices (5 per inch or less), discarding hard ends. Slice onions a bit thinner. Put both into bowl and cover with pickling salt. Mix so all slices are covered and allow to stand for at least 30 minutes. Combine cucumbers, onions, juice, and seasonings in large nonaluminum kettle. (Discard liquid that comes off cucumbers and onions as you transfer them to kettle.) Heat to boiling and boil for about 5 minutes, until slices look slightly transparent. Pack immediately in clean, hot jars; seal with hot lids. Process in water bath for 15 minutes after water returns to boiling, or in pressure cooker for 15 minutes at 10 pounds pressure. Makes 4 pints.
Variations: Cauliflower, celery stalks, carrot strips or slices, and green pepper slices all make good pickles. Prepare as above, except process for 25 minutes in boiling water bath or 20 minutes in pressure cooker.

Nutritional value: ¼ cup contains 32 Calories (P0,F0,C8). ¼ cup equals 1 diabetic vegetable exchange or ½ bread exchange. These should not be eaten by those who are on a low sodium diet, as this recipe will not succeed without salt.

Dilled Mushroom and Zucchini Pickles

Hot peppers or chili peppers (red or green)   3 to 6
White vinegar   1 quart
Water   1 cup
Noniodized pickling salt or salt substitute   ½ cup
Dill   3 teaspoons
Mushrooms   3 cups, in ¼-inch slices
Zucchini   3 cups, in ⅛-inch slices
Small garlic cloves   6

Remove stems and seeds from peppers; cut in half if using 3. Combine vinegar, water, and salt in saucepan; bring to boil and keep hot. Place ¼ teaspoon dill in bottom of each of 6 sterilized pint jars. Pack mushroom and zucchini slices into jars, and add 1 garlic clove and ½ to 1 hot pepper per jar. Pour hot vinegar liquid over vegetables, leaving at least 1 inch at the top; add remaining ¼ teaspoon dill per jar and secure lids. Process in hot water bath for 30 minutes after water returns to boiling. Allow to age several weeks before opening. Serve chilled as relish, garnish, or finger food. Makes 6 pints.

Nutritional value: ½ cup contains 28 Calories (P2,F0,C5). ½ cup equals 1 diabetic vegetable exchange. If made with salt substitute, ½ cup will contain 3 milligrams sodium.

Mustard Pickles

Cucumbers   (tiny, 2 inches or less) 2 quarts
Pearl onions   (tiny, white) 2 quarts
Green beans   2 quarts, trimmed, cut into thirds
Green tomatoes   2 quarts, quartered
Cauliflower   2 heads, cut into 1-inch buds
White cabbage   1 small head, coarsely chopped (optional)
Green peppers   6 small, coarsely chopped
Pickling salt   ¼ cup
Turmeric powder   3 tablespoons (1 ounce)
Concentrated apple juice   2 cups (4 cups simmered down)
Cider vinegar   2 cups (more as needed)
Whole mustard seed   2 tablespoons
Celery seed   2 tablespoons
Whole cloves   ½ tablespoon
Whole allspice   1 tablespoon
Dry mustard   ⅔ cup
Whole wheat flour   ¾ cup
Lemon juice   ¼ cup (plus water if needed to dissolve flour)
Date sugar   ¼ cup (optional) or
    Honey   ⅛ cup or to taste (optional)

Place cut vegetables in deep bowl, cover with salt, and mix so pickling salt is evenly distributed. Place a weighted plate over vegetables so they will stay down in bowl; let stand 24 hours. Drain, discarding liquid. Place apple juice and vinegar in large nonaluminum kettle and simmer to reduce volume even further—to about 3 cups total. Pour over drained vegetables and add spices and enough vinegar to completely cover. Place over heat and bring to a boil. Boil for 5 minutes or until vegetables are slightly soft but not mushy. Drain liquid and save. Make a thick paste with flour, lemon juice, and water. Add to liquid and cook until slightly thickened. Add vegetables (and sweetening, if desired) and heat through. Pack into clean, hot jars, cap with hot lids. Process for 15 minutes in boiling water bath after water returns to boiling, or in pressure cooker for 15 minutes (12 for crisper vegetables) at 10 pounds pressure. Makes 8 quarts, depending upon the size you cut the vegetables.
Variations: Almost any vegetable can be pickled in this mixture. Try broccoli buds, zucchini slices, or chunks of yellow summer squash. It is also good made with wax beans and small pickling onions.

Nutritional value: ¼ cup contains 28 Calories (P0,F0,C6). ¼ cup is equal to 1 diabetic vegetable exchange or ½ diabetic bread exchange. These should not be eaten by those who are on a low sodium diet, as this recipe will not succeed without salt.

Pickled Onions

Small white onions   5 cups
Salt or salt substitute   6 tablespoons
Hot water   1 quart
Pickling vinegar (distilled) 1 quart
Concentrated apple juice   ¼ cup
Lemon juice   1 tablespoon
Whole black peppercorns   1½ teaspoons
Whole cloves   1½ teaspoons
Whole allspice   1½ teaspoons

Place onions in hot water for 10 minutes, then remove outer skins. Drain and discard water. Add salt and onions to quart of hot water. Allow to stand for 12 hours. Drain and discard liquid, placing onions in sterile jars. Combine vinegar, juices, and spices. Simmer for 1 hour. Pour boiling syrup over onions and cap with sterile lids. Process in boiling water bath for 20 minutes, or in pressure cooker for 20 minutes at 10 pounds pressure. Makes 3 pints.

Nutritional value: ¼ cup contains 14 Calories (P0,F0,C3½). ¾ cup equals 1 diabetic fruit exchange or ½ cup equals 1 diabetic vegetable exchange. If this recipe is made with salt substitute instead of salt, ¼ cup contains 3 milligrams sodium.

Pickled Peaches

Small peaches, eating-ripe   8
White vinegar (distilled)   1 cup
Concentrated white grape juice   2 cups (simmered down from 4 cups)
Lemon juice   2 tablespoons
Cinnamon sticks   2, broken into pieces
Whole cloves   1 teaspoon

Drop fruit into boiling water for 1 minute, then into cold. Skins should peel off easily. Cut into halves and remove pits, saving 2 for each jar of peaches. Place remaining ingredients in nonaluminum kettle and bring to a boil. Reduce heat and gently drop in peaches, a few at a time. Simmer over low heat until fruit is tender, about 10 minutes. Drain, pack peach halves in hot, clean jars (add a couple of pits for flavor), and cover with hot liquid, leaving ¾ inch at the top for expansion. Seal with hot lids and process in boiling water bath for 20 minutes after water has returned to boiling, or in pressure cooker for 20 minutes at 5 pounds pressure. Makes 2 pints.
Variation: For brandied pickled peaches, add ½ cup brandy when finished cooking.

Nutritional value: ½ peach plus 1 tablespoon liquid contain 44 Calories (P0,F0,C11). ½ peach with juice equals 1 diabetic fruit exchange. ½ peach contains 2 milligrams sodium.

Spicy Pears

Pears, not overripe   4 pounds (10 to 12 or more)
Concentrated apple juice   1 cup
Concentrated white grape juice   1 cup (simmered down from 2 cups)
Cinnamon sticks   4 (broken into pieces)
Whole cloves   2 tablespoons
Peel from ½ large lemon   cut into strips
Ginger root   ½ inch, sliced (optional)
Pickling vinegar   1¼ cups
Red or green vegetable food coloring   ½ teaspoon (optional)

Peel, core, and halve pears. Place in deep saucepan and add juices; cover and simmer for 10 to 15 minutes until fruit is getting soft but not mushy. Place spices in small cloth bag and add to pears along with vinegar. Simmer for 5 minutes. Remove spice bag and add coloring if desired. Immediately pack into hot, clean jars, cover with hot syrup, and top with hot lids. Process in boiling water bath for 20 minutes after water returns to boiling, or in pressure cooker for 20 minutes at 5 pounds pressure. Makes 4 pints.

Nutritional value: ½ pear without syrup contains 68 Calories (P0,F0,C17), ½ pear with juice (about 1 tablespoon) contains 96 Calories (P0,F0,C24). ½ pear without juice equals 1½ diabetic fruit exchanges. If no salt is added, ½ pear with juice contains 3 milligrams sodium.

Celery Chutney

Celery   3 cups finely diced
Ripe tomatoes   6 cups chopped (or canned and omit 2 teaspoons salt)
Green pepper   ¼ cup finely diced
Medium onion   1, diced
Medium garlic clove   1, minced
Cider vinegar   ½ cup
Concentrated apple juice   ½ cup
Lemon juice   2 tablespoons
Salt or salt substitute   1 tablespoon (use 1 teaspoon if using canned
    tomatoes)
Black pepper   ½ teaspoon
Whole celery seed   1 teaspoon
Mustard seed   ½ teaspoon (optional)
Turmeric or mace   ¼ teaspoon (optional)

Combine all ingredients in large nonaluminum kettle and simmer until thick. Skim and pack immediately in clean, hot jars, leaving ¾ inch at top. Cap with hot lids. Process in boiling water bath for 10 minutes after water returns to boiling, or 10 minutes in pressure cooker at 10 pounds pressure. Makes 6 cups.

Nutritional value: 1 tablespoon contains approximately 12 Calories (P0,F0,C3). 3½ tablespoons equal 1 diabetic fruit exchange. If fresh tomatoes are used and salt substitute is used in place of salt (or omitted totally), 1 tablespoon contains 5 milligrams sodium.

Chow Chow Relish

Green tomatoes 4 cups chopped
Large onions 2, chopped
Large green peppers 2, seeded and chopped
Hot red pepper 1, seeded and chopped
Salt or salt substitute 2 teaspoons
Whole cloves 6
Bay leaf 1, broken into pieces
Cinnamon 1 teaspoon
Allspice 1 teaspoon
Dry mustard 2 teaspoons
Pickling vinegar 1 cup
Concentrated apple juice 1 cup
Horseradish 2 tablespoons (optional)

Place tomatoes, onions, and peppers in large bowl. Sprinkle with salt and leave overnight. In the morning, drain liquid and discard. Place drained vegetables in deep nonaluminum kettle. Place cloves and bay leaf in small cloth bag. Add spice bag, spices, vinegar, and apple juice to vegetables and simmer for 20 to 30 minutes until vegetables are tender and mixture has thickened. Add horseradish if desired and stir well. Remove spice bag and pack into hot, clean jars, leaving ¾ inch at top for expansion. Cap with hot lids. Process in boiling water bath for 15 minutes after water has returned to boiling, or in pressure cooker for 15 minutes at 10 pounds pressure. Makes 8 cups.

Nutritional value: 1 tablespoon contains 8 Calories (P0,F0,C2). 5 tablespoons are equal to 1 diabetic fruit exchange. If salt substitute is used in place of salt, 1 tablespoon contains 9 milligrams sodium.

Cucumber Catsup

Medium-large cucumbers 2
Large, tart apples 2 (including skin), cored and seeded
Medium onion 1
White grape juice ¼ cup
Horseradish 1 to 2 tablespoons grated
Concentrated apple juice ¼ cup
Lemon juice 2 teaspoons
Cider vinegar 1 cup
Salt or salt substitute 1½ teaspoons
Black pepper ½ teaspoon
Paprika ½ teaspoon (optional)

Grind cucumbers, apples, and onion in meat grinder using coarse blade. (A food processor makes it too fine.) Place all in deep nonaluminum kettle. Add remaining ingredients and place over heat. Bring to a boil, then turn down and cook for 8 to 10 minutes until tender. Taste and adjust seasonings if desired. Pour into hot, clean jars, leaving ¾ inch at top. Cap with hot lids and process in boiling water bath for 15 minutes after water returns to boiling, or 15 minutes in pressure cooker at 10 pounds pressure. Makes 7 cups.

Nutritional value: 1 tablespoon contains 5 Calories (P0,F0,C1¼). This can be used without replacement by a diabetic. ⅓ cup would equal 1 diabetic vegetable exchange. If made with salt substitute or without salt, this catsup contains less than 1 milligram sodium in ⅓ cup.

Pickalilli

Tomatoes (green or slightly underripe)   8 cups ground
Red sweet peppers   3 large
Green peppers   2 large
Medium onions   5
Medium apple   peeled and cored
Celery   2 cups finely chopped or ground
Salt or salt substitute   1 tablespoon
Pickling vinegar   1⅛ cups
Concentrated apple juice   1 cup
Concentrated white grape juice   ½ cup (simmered down from 1 cup)
Mustard seed   ½ teaspoon
Celery seed   ¾ teaspoon
Allspice   ½ teaspoon
White pepper   ½ teaspoon
Garlic powder   ¼ to ½ teaspoon (optional)

Grind tomatoes, peppers, onions, apple, and celery in meat grinder using coarse blade. Place in large bowl, add salt, mix well, and allow to stand overnight. In the morning, drain and discard liquid. Place in large nonaluminum kettle and add remaining ingredients. Bring to a boil, then cook slowly for 1 hour, stirring frequently. If not thick enough, continue cooking up to 30 minutes longer. Pour into hot, clean jars, leaving ¾ inch at top. Cap with hot lids and process in boiling water bath for 10 minutes after water returns to boiling, or in pressure cooker for 10 minutes at 10 pounds pressure. Makes 15 cups.

Nutritional value: 1 tablespoon contains 4 Calories (P0,F0,C1). 10 tablespoons equal 1 diabetic fruit exchange. If no salt is added, 1 tablespoon contains less than 2 milligrams sodium.

Tomato Jam
(an old Australian recipe)

Ripe tomatoes 4 pounds
Large lemons 3
Concentrated apple juice 4 cups
Allspice ¼ teaspoon or
    Ginger and mace ¼ teaspoon each
Salt or salt substitute 1 teaspoon (optional)

Peel and chop tomatoes. Place in deep nonaluminum kettle. Peel lemons as thinly as possible; cut peel into shreds. Squeeze lemons; add juice and shredded peel to tomatoes. Add juice, spice, and salt and simmer until thick. Pack into clean, hot jars, cover with hot lids, and process in boiling water bath for 10 minutes after the water returns to boiling, or in pressure cooker for 10 minutes at 5 pounds pressure. Makes 10 cups.
Variations: Green tomatoes and oranges can be substituted for some of the lemons (2 oranges plus 1 lemon). The flavor is different, but the nutritional value is the same.

Nutritional value: 1 tablespoon contains 4 Calories and can be used without replacement by diabetics. ¼ cup (P0,F0,C8) equals 1 diabetic vegetable exchange or ½ diabetic bread exchange. If made without salt, ¼ cup contains 2 milligrams sodium.

Spanish Barbecue Sauce

Tomatoes 4 cups chopped or ground
Green pepper ¼ cup seeded, chopped, or ground
Onion ½ cup peeled, chopped, or ground
Dry mustard ½ teaspoon
Salt or salt substitute 1 teaspoon
White grape juice ¾ cup
Lemon juice 2 tablespoons
Tabasco sauce ⅛ teaspoon
Cayenne pepper several sprinkles

Grind or chop vegetables as directed. Place in deep nonaluminum kettle; add remaining ingredients. Simmer for 20 minutes or until mixture is thick. (Put through food mill to remove seeds, if desired.) Pack into hot, clean jars, leaving ¾ inch at top. Cap with hot lids. To freeze, set aside to cool and freeze in sharp freeze area of freezer until hard. To can, process in boiling water bath for 15 minutes after water has returned to boiling, or in pressure cooker for 15 minutes at 10 pounds pressure. Makes 3 cups.

Nutritional value: 1 tablespoon contains 6 Calories (P0,F0,C1½). 4½ tablespoons equal 1 diabetic fruit exchange. If no salt is added, 1 tablespoon contains about 4 milligrams sodium.

Tomato Catsup

Large, ripe tomatoes   12, peeled and cored
Large onions   2, peeled, finely chopped
Large green peppers   4, seeded, finely chopped
Pickling vinegar   4 cups
Concentrated apple juice   1 cup
Lemon juice   1½ tablespoons
Salt or salt substitute   2 tablespoons
Ginger   1 tablespoon
Cinnamon   1 tablespoon
Mustard   1 tablespoon
Nutmeg   1 teaspoon
Black pepper   ½ teaspoon

Place all ingredients in deep nonaluminum kettle. Bring to a boil and simmer until thick (about 3 hours). Skim and pack immediately in hot, clean jars, leaving ¾ inch at top. Cap with hot lids. Process for 10 minutes in boiling water bath after water has returned to boiling, or in pressure cooker for 10 minutes at 10 pounds pressure. Makes 8 cups.

Nutritional value: 1 tablespoon contains 8 Calories (P0,F0,C2). 5 tablespoons equal 1 diabetic fruit exchange. If salt substitute is used or salt omitted, 1 tablespoon contains 2 milligrams sodium.

Winter Recipes

Canning and preserving don't have to be limited to summer months. Foods are available all year long that can be used to make good jams, jellies, and pickles. Citrus fruits (their peak season is during the winter, not summer), winter pears, winter grapes, late fall apples, cabbage, cucumbers, celery, green peppers, and onions are in the market year round. So you see there are a number of foods that can be used, plus the frozen fruits and vegetables which we can buy all year. They will be more expensive than if purchased in season, but they will still taste good.

I have called these "Winter" recipes, but they are really "Year-Round" treats, and can be made any time with what is normally in the grocery store.

Christmastime Marmalade

Medium grapefruit 1, seeded, with juice
Whole orange 1, seeded, with juice
Oranges 3 (pulp only), seeded, with juice
Tangerine 1, seeded, with juice
Lemon ½, seeded, with juice
Concentrated apple juice 1½ cups
White grape juice ½ cup
Lemon juice 3 tablespoons
Unflavored gelatin 1 tablespoon (1 envelope)
Low methoxy pectin solution 1 cup
Calcium solution 5 teaspoons
Salt dash (optional)

Slice all fruit very thin, including rinds, except from 3 oranges. Place all fruit in deep nonaluminum kettle, add juices, and simmer until cooked and rinds look translucent. Add small amount of water if needed to keep from getting too thick while cooking. Remove from heat and sprinkle gelatin over hot liquid, stirring well to be sure it dissolves. Add pectin solution, calcium solution, and salt; reheat to boiling. Pour into hot, clean jars, leaving ¾ inch at top. Cap with hot lids and process in boiling water bath for 10 minutes after water has returned to boiling, or in pressure cooker for 10 minutes at 5 pounds pressure. Makes 6½ cups.

Nutritional value: 1 tablespoon contains 18 Calories (P0,F0,C4½). 2 tablespoons equal 1 diabetic fruit exchange. If no salt is added, 2 tablespoons contain less than 1 milligram sodium.

Frostberry Jam

Whole frozen berries   2 cups
White grape juice   1 cup
Lemon juice   2½ tablespoons
Lemon rind   ¼ teaspoon grated
Low methoxy pectin solution   ½ cup
Salt   dash (optional)
Calcium solution   2½ teaspoons

Place frozen berries, juices, and rind in a deep nonaluminum kettle. Simmer until berries are barely cooked—about 5 minutes. Mash berries to break up any large pieces. Add pectin and salt and stir. Return to heat, bring to a boil, then add calcium solution and remix. Skim and pour into hot, sterile jars, leaving ¾ inch at top. Cap with hot, sterile lids. If any jars fail to seal, process in boiling water bath for 10 minutes after water has returned to boiling, or in pressure cooker for 10 minutes at 5 pounds pressure. If any still fail to seal, refrigerate and use within 10 days. Makes 3½ cups.

Nutritional value: 1 tablespoon contains 8 Calories (P0,F0,C2). 5 tablespoons equal 1 diabetic fruit exchange. If no salt is added, 2 tablespoons contain less than 1 milligram sodium.

Jam-Pot Jam

Odds and ends of fruit* (canned peaches, apricots, pears, etc.)   3 cups
White grape juice   1 cup
Lemon juice   2 tablespoons
Lemon   1 slice, seeded and chopped
Whole cloves   6 to 8 (optional)
Low methoxy pectin solution   ½ cup
Calcium solution   2½ teaspoons
Salt   dash (optional)

Drain fruit, saving juice, and chop into small pieces. Place fruit, juice drained from it before chopping, other juices, lemon, and cloves in deep saucepan. Simmer until fruit is very soft and lemon pieces are translucent. Add pectin, calcium solution, and salt; stir well. Return to heat and bring to a boil. Pour into hot, clean jars, leaving ¾ inch at top. Process in boiling water bath for 10 minutes after water returns to boiling, or in pressure cooker for 10 minutes at 5 pounds pressure. Makes 3 cups.
* Accumulate in a jar in refrigerator, adding remains of various fruits until there is enough for a batch of jam. Each batch will be different and, of course, allspice, nutmeg, and other spices can be added to suit your taste.

Nutritional value: 1 tablespoon contains 8 to 12 Calories (P0,F0,C2-3), depending on fruits used. 3½ to 5 tablespoons equal 1 diabetic fruit exchange. If no salt is added, 1 tablespoon will contain less than 1 milligram sodium.

Mother's Carrot Jam

Carrots   2 cups peeled and chopped
Concentrated apple juice   2 cups
Date sugar   4 tablespoons or
    Honey   ¼ cup
Lemons   2, juice and grated rind
Almonds   ½ cup, blanched and chopped
Salt   dash (optional)

Place carrots in saucepan; cover with water. Cook until tender. Drain, discarding water. Place with other ingredients in deep kettle. Simmer until thick. Taste. If not sweet enough, add more date sugar or honey, being careful not to overpower taste of fruit. Add nuts and reheat for 2 to 3 minutes. Pour into sterile pint jars, leaving ¾ inch at top. Cover with hot lids. Process in boiling water bath for 10 minutes after water returns to boiling, or in pressure cooker for 10 minutes at 5 pounds pressure. Makes 4 cups.

Nutritional value: 4 tablespoons jam made with date sugar contain 62 Calories (P1,F2,C10). ¼ cup equals 1 diabetic fruit exchange plus ½ diabetic fat exchange. *Diabetics and hypoglycemics should not use jam made with honey.* If made without adding salt, 4 tablespoons contain 7 milligrams sodium.

Pineapple Jam

Crushed or chunk-style pineapple   1 cup (in own juice)
Canned pineapple juice   ¾ cup
Lemon juice   1 tablespoon
Lemon rind   ¼ teaspoon grated
Low methoxy pectin solution   ½ cup
Calcium solution   2½ teaspoons
Salt   dash (optional)

Place pineapple in blender and blend until no large chunks are left. Combine with other juices and rind in a deep nonaluminum saucepan. Heat until boiling. Add pectin solution and bring to a boil again. Remove from heat and add calcium solution. Mix well. Pour into clean, hot jars, leaving ¾ inch at top for expansion. Cap with hot lids. Process in a boiling water bath for 10 minutes after the water has returned to boiling, or in pressure cooker for 10 minutes at 5 pounds pressure. If any jars do not seal, refrigerate and use within 10 days. Makes 2½ cups.

Nutritional value: 2 tablespoons contain 16 Calories (P0,F0,C4). 5 tablespoons equal 1 diabetic fruit exchange. If no salt is added, 5 tablespoons contain less than 1 milligram sodium.

Tomato-Pineapple Jam

Canned whole tomatoes with juice   2 cups chopped
Crushed pineapple   1 cup (in own juice)
Lemon juice   2 tablespoons
Concentrated apple juice   1 cup
White grape juice   ½ cup
Lemon slices   2, seeded and minced
Cream of tartar   1/16 teaspoon

Place tomatoes with juice in deep nonaluminum kettle. Add pineapple, juices, and lemon slices. Boil for an hour or longer over low heat, until thickened. Stir often to prevent sticking. Remove from heat and add cream of tartar, stirring well to dissolve. Skim and pour into hot, clean jars, leaving ¾ inch at top. Cap with hot lids and process in boiling water bath for 20 minutes after water returns to boiling, or in pressure cooker for 20 minutes at 10 pounds pressure. Makes 2½ cups.

Nutritional value: 1 tablespoon contains 16 Calories (P0,F0,C4). 2½ tablespoons equal 1 diabetic fruit exchange. If no salt is added and salt-free canned tomatoes are used, 1 tablespoon will contain 1 milligram sodium.

Cranberry Jelly

Cranberries   2 cups
Concentrated apple juice   1 cup
Lemon juice   ¼ cup
Liquid pectin (regular)   3 ounces (½ package)
Glycerine   5 tablespoons
Gelatin   1 tablespoon (1 envelope)

Wash and pick over cranberries, discarding any that are soft. Place in a deep saucepan and add fruit juices. Cover and simmer for about 20 minutes, until fruit is soft. Mash to break up any berries left whole. Strain in food mill to remove seeds. Return to saucepan and heat to boiling. Add pectin, glycerine, and gelatin, stirring well to dissolve gelatin, and boil for 1 minute. Remove from heat, skim, and pour into hot, clean jars, leaving ¾ inch at top. Cap with hot lids. Process in boiling water bath for 10 minutes after water has returned to boiling, or in pressure cooker for 10 minutes at 5 pounds pressure. Makes 3 cups.
Variation: You can substitute ½ cup low methoxy pectin solution and

2½ teaspoons calcium solution for the liquid pectin, glycerine, and gelatin.

Nutritional value: 1 tablespoon contains 20 Calories (P0,F0,C5). 2 tablespoons equal 1 diabetic fruit exchange. If no salt is added, 2 tablespoons contain 1 milligram sodium.

Grape Jelly

Unsweetened grape juice   3 cups (2 cups Concord plus 1 cup white grape)
Lemon juice   1 tablespoon
Low methoxy pectin solution   ½ cup
Calcium solution   2½ teaspoons
Salt   dash (optional)

Simmer grape juice down to 2 cups, then add lemon juice and pectin solution. Bring to a boil, remove from heat, and add calcium solution and salt. Stir well. Pour into hot, clean jars, leaving ¾ inch at top. Cap with hot lids. Process in boiling water bath for 10 minutes after water returns to boiling, or in pressure cooker 10 minutes at 5 pounds pressure. If any jar still does not seal, refrigerate and use within 10 days. Makes 2½ cups.

Nutritional value: 1 tablespoon contains 16 Calories (P0,F0,C4). 2½ tablespoons equal 1 diabetic fruit exchange. If made without added salt, 2 tablespoons contain less than 1 milligram sodium.

Wine Jelly

Wine (Sherry, Tokay, or Chablis)   2 cups
Concentrated apple juice   ½ cup
Lemon juice   2 tablespoons
Low methoxy pectin solution   ¾ cup
Calcium solution   scant 4 teaspoons
Salt   dash (optional)

Combine all liquids in deep saucepan, bring to a boil, and add low methoxy pectin, calcium solution, and salt. Stir well to dissolve. Pour into hot, clean jars, leaving ¾ inch at top. Cap with hot lids and process in boiling water bath for 10 minutes after water returns to boiling, or in pressure cooker for 10 minutes at 5 pounds pressure. Makes 3 cups.

Nutritional value: Made with dry wine, 1 tablespoon contains 15 Calories (P0,F0,C2, Alcohol 7 Calories). 2½ tablespoons equal 1 diabetic fruit exchange. *This should not be used by hypoglycemics.* If no salt is added, 1 tablespoon contains less than 1 milligram sodium.

Herb Jelly

Herb Infusion   2 cups
Cider vinegar   ¼ cup
Concentrated apple juice   2 cups
Lemon juice   2 tablespoons
Low methoxy pectin solution   1 cup
Calcium solution   5 teaspoons
Green vegetable coloring   ¼ teaspoon (optional)

Place 2 cups herb infusion, vinegar, and juices in deep nonaluminum kettle. Stir in pectin and heat to boiling. Add calcium solution and coloring; mix well. Pour into hot, clean jars, leaving ¾ inch at top. Cap with hot lids. Process in boiling water bath for 10 minutes after water returns to boiling, or 10 minutes in pressure cooker at 5 pounds pressure. Makes 5½ cups.

Nutritional value: 1 tablespoon contains 12 Calories (P0,F0,C3). 3½ tablespoons equal 1 diabetic fruit exchange. If no salt is added, ½ cup contains 1 milligram sodium.

Herb Infusion

Pour 2½ cups boiling water over 4 tablespoons dried or 1 cup fresh chopped herbs, leaves, and stems (use basil, marjoram, rosemary, thyme, or Italian herb mix). Let stand 15 to 20 minutes. Strain through fine strainer to remove herbs. Makes 2½ cups.

Mint Jelly

Apple juice   2 cups
Lemon juice   1 tablespoon
Mint extract   ¼ teaspoon or
    Fresh mint   2 large sprigs
Green vegetable coloring   ¼ teaspoon (optional)
Low methoxy pectin solution   ½ cup
Calcium solution   2½ teaspoons

Place apple juice, lemon juice, and mint in saucepan and bring to a quick boil. Add green food color and pectin. Stir well to dissolve; return to heat and bring liquids to a boil. Remove from heat and add calcium solution. Stir well. Pour into clean, hot jars, leaving ¾ inch at top. Cap with hot lids. Process in boiling water bath for 10 minutes after water returns to boiling, or 10 minutes at 5 pounds pressure in a pressure cooker. Makes 2½ cups.

Variations: This jelly can be flavored with other herbs as well. Try geranium leaves, or sprigs of thyme, or rosemary.

Nutritional value: 1 tablespoon contains 8 Calories (P0,F0,C2). 5 tablespoons equal 1 diabetic fruit exchange. If no salt is added, 5 tablespoons contain less than 1 milligram sodium.

Dried Apricot-Pineapple Preserves

Crushed pineapple   1 cup (in own juice), drained
Large lemon   ¼ to ⅓, finely chopped (including juice)
Canned pineapple juice   1 cup
Dried apricots   1½ pounds, diced
Salt   dash (optional)

Drain pineapple, set aside; add pineapple juice to other juices, use to soak apricots, adding enough water to cover fruit. Soak at least 2 hours (overnight is even better), then place in deep saucepan and simmer for 20 minutes, stirring often. Add remaining ingredients and continue to cook until thick. Taste, adding more lemon if desired. Remove from heat and pack into sterile half-pint jars, leaving ¾ inch at top. Cap with sterile lids screwed down firmly. To freeze, cool to room temperature, then place in sharp freeze section of freezer until hard. Remove to other shelf for storage. To can, process in boiling water bath for 10 minutes after water returns to boiling, or in pressure cooker 10 minutes at 5 pounds pressure. Makes 3½ to 4 cups.

Variations: Use mixtures of dried fruits to vary the flavor of these preserves; for example, dried peaches in place of half the apricots.

Nutritional value: 1 tablespoon contains 28 Calories (P0,F0,C7). 1½ tablespoons equal 1 diabetic fruit exchange. If no salt is added, 3 tablespoons contain less than 1 milligram sodium.

Dried Peach Preserves

Dried peaches 2 pounds, coarsely chopped
Apple-pear juice 3½ cups
Lemon juice 3 tablespoons
Orange juice ¾ cup
Seedless raisins 1 cup chopped
Orange 1, sliced paper thin, seeded
Salt dash (optional)
Walnuts or pecans 1 cup chopped

Soak dried peaches in juices overnight. In the morning, place in deep nonaluminum pan and add remaining ingredients except chopped nuts. Cook over low heat until thick, stirring frequently to prevent sticking. Add nuts and remove from heat. Pour into hot, clean half-pint jars, leaving ¾ inch at top. Cap with hot lids. Process in boiling water bath for 10 minutes after water returns to boiling, or in pressure cooker for 10 minutes at 5 pounds pressure. Makes 8½ to 9 cups.

Nutritional value: 1 tablespoon contains 27 Calories (P0,F½,C5½). 5 teaspoons equal 1 diabetic fruit exchange. If made without added salt, 1 tablespoon contains less than 1 milligram sodium.

Extra Good Apricot Butter

Dried apricots 1 pound
White grape juice 1 cup
Concentrated apple juice 1 cup
Lemon juice 2 tablespoons
Large lemon 1, seeded and chopped
Cinnamon 1 teaspoon
Cloves ½ teaspoon
Allspice ¼ teaspoon (optional)
Salt dash (optional)

Soak dried fruit overnight in fruit juices with enough water added to cover. In morning, add chopped lemon and place in blender to soften hard pieces. Cook over low heat until fruit tastes cooked, about 8 minutes. Add spices and simmer until thick, about 10 minutes longer. Pour into hot, clean jars, leaving ¾ inch at top. Cap with hot lids and process in boiling water bath for 10 minutes after water returns to boiling, or in pressure cooker for 10 minutes at 5 pounds pressure. To freeze, cool covered jars to room temperature, then place in sharp freeze section of freezer. When hard, move to other area of freezer for storage. To use, thaw overnight in refrigerator. Makes 5 cups.

Nutritional value: 1 tablespoon contains 16 Calories (P0,F0,C4). 2½ tablespoons equal 1 diabetic fruit exchange. If no salt is added, 1 tablespoon contains 2 milligrams sodium.

Lemony Prune Butter

Medium prunes ¾ cup
Concentrated apple juice 1 cup
Large lemon ¼, finely chopped or ground, with juice
Cinnamon ½ to 1 teaspoon (add ½ when cooking)
Salt dash (optional)

Soak prunes overnight in apple juice. Drain, saving liquid. Remove pits. Place prunes in a deep nonaluminum saucepan; add remaining ingredients and reserved liquid. Simmer over low heat until thickened, mashing to break up any prune pieces, if needed. Taste. Add more cinnamon if stronger flavor is desired. When thickened, pour into sterile jars, leaving ¾ inch at top. Cap with sterile lids, screwed down firmly. To freeze, cool to room temperature, then place in sharp freeze section of freezer until hard. Move to other shelf for storage. To can, process in boiling water bath for 10 minutes after water returns to boiling, or in pressure cooker for 10 minutes at 5 pounds pressure. Makes 2¼ cups. **Variations:** Try the spice combination suggested for Apple Butter, but in reduced amounts, or try adding nutmeg.

Nutritional value: 1 tablespoon contains 24 Calories (P0,F0,C6). 1½ tablespoons equal 1 diabetic fruit exchange. If no salt is added, 2 tablespoons contain less than 1 milligram sodium.

Raisin-Apple Spread

Seedless raisins   1 cup
Boiling water   2 tablespoons
Concentrated apple juice   ¼ cup, boiling hot
Lemon juice   2 tablespoons
Unsweetened applesauce (see Index)   1 cup
Cinnamon   ½ teaspoon
Cloves   ¼ teaspoon
Lemon rind   ½ teaspoon grated
Salt   dash (optional)

Soak raisins in water and juices for at least 15 minutes. Put into blender and run at medium speed until all are pureed. Combine with remaining ingredients and cook over low heat until quite thick, stirring often to prevent sticking. Taste. Add more spices if desired. Pour into hot, clean jars, leaving ¾ inch at top. Cap with hot lids. Either cool and sharp freeze or process in boiling water bath for 10 minutes after water returns to boiling, or in pressure cooker for 10 minutes at 5 pounds pressure. Makes 2 cups.

Nutritional value: 1 tablespoon contains 20 Calories (P0,F0,C5). 2 tablespoons equal 1 diabetic fruit exchange. If no salt is added, 2 tablespoons contain less than 1 milligram sodium.

Australian Tomato Sauce
(like catsup)

Canned whole tomatoes with juice   6 cups chopped
Onions   1¼ cups peeled and chopped or coarsely ground
Large garlic clove   1, peeled and minced or ground
White grape juice   1½ cups
Cider vinegar   ½ cup
Cloves   ½ tablespoon
Ginger   1 teaspoon
Salt or salt substitute   1½ teaspoons

Place chopped or coarsely ground vegetables in deep nonaluminum kettle. Add remaining ingredients and cook over low heat until thick. Remove from heat, skim, and put through food mill. Return to heat and bring to a boil. Pack into hot, clean jars, leaving 1 inch at top. Cap with hot lids and process in boiling water bath for 20 minutes after water returns to boiling, or in pressure cooker for 20 minutes at 10 pounds pressure. Makes 6 cups.

Nutritional value: ¼ cup contains 20 Calories (P1,F0,C4). ⅓ cup equals 1 diabetic vegetable exchange. If no salt is added or salt substitute is used, ¼ cup contains less than 3 milligams sodium.

Marinated Mushrooms and Zucchini Slices

Zucchini 1½ cups thinly sliced
Small mushrooms 1½ cups cut in half
Marinade

Place zucchini and mushrooms in 1-quart plastic container with tight lid. Pour marinade over them, cover, and refrigerate at least 6 hours to chill and blend flavors. Stir often to ensure that all vegetables are well covered with liquid. Drain; serve with toothpicks. Makes 3 cups.

Marinade

Garlic clove 1, bruised
Vegetable oil 3 tablespoons
White vinegar ½ cup
Honey ⅓ teaspoon or
    Concentrated apple juice 1½ teaspoons
Tabasco sauce 3 to 4 drops

Rub small bowl with garlic; place garlic in bowl, add remaining ingredients, and mix well.

Nutritional value: ½ cup contains 43 Calories (P1,F3,C3). 1 cup equals 1 diabetic fat exchange and 1 vegetable exchange. ½ cup contains 2 milligrams sodium.

Delicious Pickled Vegetable Salad

Concentrated apple juice ¼ cup
Cider vinegar ⅔ cup
Salt or salt substitute 1 teaspoon
Celery seeds 1 teaspoon
Mustard seeds ½ teaspoon
Cabbage 1 cup grated coarsely
Canned beets 1 cup minced
Onion ¼ cup minced
Green pepper ¼ cup minced
Celery ¼ cup minced

Combine juice, vinegar, salt, and seeds. Bring to a boil, cook for 5 minutes. Add vegetables, stir, lower heat, and simmer for 10 minutes. Pour into hot, clean jars, leaving 1 inch at top. Cap with hot lids and process for 20 minutes after water returns to boiling, or in pressure cooker for 20 minutes at 10 pounds pressure. Makes 3 cups.

Nutritional value: ½ cup contains 28 Calories (P1,F0,C6). ¾ cup equals 1 diabetic vegetable exchange. If salt substitute and diet-pack beets are used, ½ cup contains 24 milligrams sodium.

Sweet-and-Sour Cabbage Pickle
(Cabbage Tsukemono)

Concentrated apple juice 1½ cups
Cider vinegar 3 tablespoons
Coarse pickling salt 2 tablespoons
Sherry or dry white wine 3 tablespoons
Cabbage 12 cups cut into 1-inch pieces

Combine all ingredients except cabbage in nonaluminum saucepan; bring to a boil and boil until salt is dissolved. Cool slightly and pour over cabbage. Press cabbage down with plate on which a heavy weight is placed (glass jar filled with water will work). Allow to stand 24 hours. Drain and serve. Makes 6 cups.
Note: This does not can well; use fresh only.

Nutritional value: ¼ cup contains 28 Calories (P0,F0,C7). ¼ cup equals 1 diabetic vegetable exchange. This recipe cannot be made satisfactorily with salt substitute. It should not be used on low salt diets.

Mother's Beet-Cabbage Relish

Cabbage 4 cups chopped
Canned beets 4 cups chopped
Concentrated white grape juice 1 cup (simmered down from 3 cups) or
    Water ¾ cup and
    Honey ¼ cup
Lemon juice 1 tablespoon
Horseradish 1 cup grated
Vinegar 1 cup
Pepper 1 tablespoon
Salt or salt substitute 1 teaspoon
Cayenne pepper ¼ teaspoon

Combine all ingredients; bring to a boil. Pack into clean, hot jars, leaving 1 inch at the top for expansion. Top with hot lids. Process in boiling water bath for 20 minutes after water returns to boiling, or in pressure cooker for 15 minutes at 10 pounds pressure. Keep refrigerated after opening. Makes 9 cups.
Note: This is delicious with cold meat and makes a colorful and tasty garnish for luncheon or dinner dishes.

Nutritional value: 1 tablespoon contains 8 Calories (P0,F0,C2). Can be used without replacement by diabetics. ¼ cup relish is equal to 1 diabetic vegetable exchange (C8) or ½ diabetic bread exchange. If salt substitute is used, 1 tablespoon contains 2 milligrams sodium.

Pickled Beet Slices

Canned beet slices   7 cups
Cider vinegar   1½ cups
Concentrated apple juice   1½ cups
Lemon juice   1 tablespoon
Whole cloves   2 tablespoons
Large cinnamon stick   1, broken into 4 pieces

Drain canned beets, discarding liquid. Fill 4 hot, clean jars with beet slices, leaving 1 inch at top. Combine all ingredients and bring to a boil. Divide spices evenly among jars. Pour hot liquid over beets, adding small amount of boiling water if needed to fill jars. Cap with hot lids and process for 20 minutes after water returns to boiling, or in pressure cooker for 20 minutes at 10 pounds pressure. Makes 7 cups.

Nutritional value: 3 tablespoons (scant ¼ cup) contain 28 Calories (P1,F0,C6). 3 tablespoons equal 1 diabetic vegetable exchange. If made with freshly cooked or diet-packed canned beets, 3 tablespoons contain 22 milligrams sodium.

Pickled Eggs

Apple juice   ¾ cup
Whole mixed pickling spices   ½ teaspoon
Salt or salt substitute   ½ teaspoon
Celery seeds   ¼ teaspoon
Mustard seeds   ⅛ teaspoon
Cider vinegar   1 cup
Water   ½ cup
Garlic clove   ½, minced
Eggs   6, hard-cooked, shelled

Combine all ingredients except eggs in deep nonaluminum saucepan. Simmer for 10 minutes. Prick eggs with fork to make design around middle and ends. Pour hot liquid over eggs and allow to stand at room temperature before placing in refrigerator. Let stand 48 hours or longer before using. Serve whole or halved as appetizer or salad garnish. Makes 6. **Note:** These taste like deviled eggs.

Nutritional value: 1 egg contains 86 Calories (P7,F6,C1), and equals 1 diabetic meat exchange. If salt substitute is used, 1 egg contains 72 milligrams sodium.

Pickled Green Beans

Frozen green beans, julienne cut   two 10-ounce packages
Large garlic cloves   2
Thin lemon slice   1, chopped
Onion   ½ cup thinly sliced
Cider vinegar   1 cup
Apple juice   ¼ cup
Large bay leaf   1, broken into pieces
Salt or salt substitute   ½ teaspoon
Whole pickling spice   ½ teaspoon
Whole allspice   ¼ teaspoon
Whole mustard seeds   ¼ teaspoon

Cover beans with boiling water and cook 5 minutes. Drain, saving liquid. Pack into clean, hot jars. Combine remaining ingredients with bean liquid and simmer for 8 minutes. Pour over beans, adding boiling water if needed to bring liquid to within 1 inch of top of jar. Cover with hot lids, process in boiling water bath for 20 minutes after water returns to boiling, or in pressure cooker for 20 minutes at 10 pounds pressure. Makes 4 cups.

Nutritional value: ½ cup contains 24 calories (P1,F0,C5). ¾ cup equals 1 diabetic vegetable exchange. If salt substitute is used, ½ cup contains 51 milligrams sodium.

Pineapple Pickles

Distilled vinegar   ⅝ cup
Concentrated apple juice   ½ cup
Lemon juice   1 tablespoon
Pineapple juice   ¾ cup (juice drained from fruit, plus extra if needed)
Whole cloves   1½ teaspoons
Cinnamon stick   1, broken into 4 pieces
Pineapple chunks   16-ounce can (in own juice), drained

Boil vinegar, juices, cloves, and cinnamon together for 10 minutes. Add drained pineapple and simmer for 20 minutes. Pack into hot, clean jars, leaving 1 inch at the top. Add more pineapple juice if needed to cover fruit. Cap with hot lids and process in boiling water bath for 15 minutes after water returns to boiling, or in pressure cooker for 15 minutes at 5 pounds pressure. Makes 2 pints.

Nutritional value: ⅓ cup contains 36 Calories (P0,F0,C9). ⅓ cup equals 1 diabetic fruit exchange. ⅓ cup contains 1 milligram sodium.

Hot Pickled Mushrooms

Small button mushrooms   1 pound
Large garlic cloves   3, peeled and sliced
Dried hot red pepper   1 tablespoon (2 tablespoons if you like them hot)
Whole peppercorns   ¼ teaspoon
Large bay leaves   3, broken into pieces
Distilled vinegar   1 cup
Water   1 cup
Apple juice   ¼ cup
Salt or salt substitute   ¾ teaspoon

Wash mushrooms and slice off and discard stem ends. Cut into halves, quartering larger ones. Place in hot, clean jars, filling half-full, then adding ⅓ sliced garlic, ⅓ red pepper and ⅓ peppercorns to each. Fill to within 1 inch of top with mushrooms. Combine all other ingredients in saucepan and bring to a boil. Pour over mushrooms, adding more hot water to each jar if needed to cover completely. Cap with hot lids and process in boiling water bath for 20 minutes after water returns to boiling, or 20 minutes in pressure cooker at 10 pounds pressure. Makes 4 cups (3 pints before cooking).

Nutritional value: ½ cup contains 40 Calories (P3,F0,C7). ½ cup equals 1 diabetic vegetable exchange. If no salt is used, ½ cup contains 6 milligrams sodium.

Spiced Apples

Concentrated apple juice   1½ cups
Distilled vinegar   ⅔ cup
Whole cloves   1 teaspoon
Cinnamon stick   1, broken into 4 pieces
Red food coloring   ⅓ teaspoon (optional)
Medium apples (sweet and firm, like Yellow Delicious)   5, peeled, cut
   into eighths

Combine all ingredients except apples in saucepan and bring to a boil. Drop apples into hot solution, and simmer until slightly soft, about 10 minutes at most. Pack into hot, clean jars, leaving ¾ inch at top. Cap with hot lids, process in boiling water bath for 5 minutes after water returns to boiling, or in pressure cooker for 15 minutes at 5 pounds pressure. Makes 2 pints.
Note: These taste like old-fashioned crabapple pickles.

Nutritional value: 3 pieces contain 36 Calories (P0,F0,C9). 3 pieces equal 1 diabetic fruit exchange. 3 pieces contain less than 2 milligrams sodium.

Tangy Fruit Relish

Large apple 1, peeled and chopped
Medium lemon 1 cup sliced paper thin
Lemon juice 3 tablespoons
Bean sprouts 1 cup coarsely chopped
Dried apricots 1 cup cooked and chopped
Raisins ¼ cup
Salt dash (optional)
Water ½ cup
Unflavored gelatin 1 tablespoon (1 envelope)

Combine all ingredients except gelatin in saucepan and cook over low heat until fruit is tender and relish thickened. Add additional water while cooking if needed to prevent sticking. Remove from heat and sprinkle gelatin over hot relish, stirring rapidly to dissolve. Adjust seasonings to taste. Pour into small sterilized jars, put on lids, and cool to room temperature before refrigerating. Makes 3 cups.
Note: This relish does not keep well and should be frozen if kept for longer than a few days. Be sure to leave ¾ inch for expansion at the top of the jars if you do plan to freeze.

Nutritional value: ¼ cup equals 24 Calories (P1,F0,C5). ¼ cup equals ½ diabetic fruit exchange. If no salt is used, ¼ cup contains 5 milligrams sodium.

Uncooked Cucumber Relish

Large cucumbers 5, peeled and seeded
Green pepper ½, seeded
Large onion 1, peeled
Medium apple (preferably tart) 1, peeled and cored
Distilled vinegar 1 cup
Salt or salt substitute 1½ teaspoons
Black pepper 1 teaspoon
Mustard seed 1 teaspoon
Celery seed ½ teaspoon
Tabasco sauce dash (optional)

Grind all vegetables and apple in meat grinder using medium blade. Mix with remaining ingredients and pack into hot, clean jars. Refrigerate until used. This will keep for several weeks in the refrigerator but it loses its crunchiness after a few days. Makes 3½ cups.

Nutritional value: ¼ cup contains 32 Calories (P1,F0,C7). ¼ cup equals 1 diabetic vegetable exchange. If made with salt substitute, ¼ cup contains 10 milligrams sodium.

Tomato Sauce

Medium onions 2, chopped
Green pepper 1, chopped
Tomato paste 4 cups or
    Tomato puree 8 cups*
Water 4 cups
Large garlic clove minced
Concentrated apple juice 1 cup
Cider vinegar ⅔ cup
Lemon juice 2 tablespoons
Salt 1 tablespoon
Black pepper ¼ teaspoon

Combine vegetables in large nonaluminum kettle. Add all other ingredients and cook over low heat until vegetables are very soft and volume is reduced by about one-third. Remove from heat and put through a food mill. Return to stove, heat to boiling. Pack in hot, clean jars with hot lids, leaving 1 inch at top. Process in boiling water bath for 15 minutes after water returns to boiling, or in pressure cooker for 15 minutes at 10 pounds pressure. To freeze, place in sharp freeze section of freezer after jars reach room temperature. Store in main freezer section. Thaw in refrigerator. Makes 6 cups.

* Omit 4 cups water and salt if tomato puree is used.

Nutritional value: 1 tablespoon contains 12 Calories (P0,F0,C3). 3½ tablespoons equal 1 diabetic fruit exchange. If tomato paste is used and no salt is added, 1 tablespoon contains less than 1 milligram sodium.

Winter Corn Relish

Frozen whole kernel corn   4 cups
Green cabbage   1½ cups finely chopped
Medium white onions   3
Green peppers   2, seeded and stem removed
Dried hot red peppers   2 tablespoons
Pimiento   ¼ cup minced
Cider vinegar   2½ cups
Concentrated apple juice   ½ cup
White grape juice   ½ cup (simmered down from 1 cup)
Salt   1 tablespoon (optional)
Celery seed   ⅔ teaspoon
Mustard seed   ⅔ teaspoon

Place corn in large nonaluminum kettle. Grind other vegetables, using coarse blade in meat grinder. Add with remaining ingredients to corn and bring to a boil. Turn down heat and simmer for 35 minutes. Skim and pack immediately into clean, hot jars. Cap with hot, sterile lids and process in boiling water bath for 20 minutes after water returns to boiling, or in pressure cooker for 20 minutes at 10 pounds pressure. Makes 8½ to 9 cups.

Nutritional value: 2 tablespoons with juice equal 16 Calories (P0,F0,C4). 5 tablespoons equal 1 diabetic fruit exchange. If no salt is used, 2 tablespoons contain 4 milligrams sodium.

Winter Tomato Catsup

Use recipe for Tomato Catsup with Honey (see Index) but omit honey, substituting ¾ cup concentrated apple juice plus 2 tablespoons extra lemon juice.

Nutritional value: 1 tablespoon contains 12 Calories (P0,F0,C3). 4 tablespoons equal 1 diabetic fruit exchange, 2 tablespoons equal 1 diabetic vegetable exchange. Sodium value does not change with this substitution.

Winter Indian Chutney

Canned tomatoes   4 cups chopped with juice
Large onions   3, peeled
Large green pepper   1, seeded
Dried hot red pepper   1½ to 2
Large, tart apples   4
Seedless raisins   ⅞ cup
Concentrated apple juice   ¼ cup (simmered down from ½ cup)
White grape juice   ¼ cup (simmered down from ½ cup)
Cider vinegar   1-1⅓ cups
Salt or salt substitute   1½ teaspoons
Curry powder   1 teaspoon (optional)

Grind all vegetables and fruit in meat grinder using medium blade. Place in deep nonaluminum kettle and add remaining ingredients. Simmer until thickened (approximately 1 hour). Skim and pack in hot, sterile jars, leaving 1 inch at top. Cap with hot, sterile lids. If any fail to seal, process in boiling water bath for 20 minutes after water returns to boiling, or in pressure cooker for 20 minutes at 10 pounds pressure. **Makes 8 cups.**

Nutritional value: 2 tablespoons contain 20 Calories (P0,F0,C5). 4 tablespoons equal 1 diabetic fruit exchange. 2 tablespoons contain 2 milligrams sodium if salt substitute and diet-pack tomatoes are used.

Other Recipes to Make Year-Round

Jams, Jellies, and Preserves:
  Apple-Berry Jam (frozen berries)
  Apricot Marmalade (dried apricots)
  Mixed Soft Fruit Jam (diet canned fruit)
  Apple Jelly (frozen apple juice)
  Orange Juice Jelly (frozen orange juice)
  Apricot-Pineapple Jam (dried apricots, canned pineapple)
  Orange-Blueberry Jam (frozen berries)
  Strawberry Date Nut Preserves (frozen berries)
  Frozen Blueberry Jam (frozen berries)
  Lazy Person's Plum Jam (dried prunes)
  Grape Jelly (canned grape juice)
  Meatless Mincemeat

Pickles and Relishes:
  Dilled Zucchini and Mushroom Pickles
  Spicy Pears (winter pears)
  Celery Chutney (canned tomatoes)
  Cucumber Catsup

Preserving with Honey

Advantages of Using Honey for Canning

Honey is manufactured by bees from nectar gathered from flowers, flowering trees, and shrubs. It can taste mild or strong, depending on the nectar and its source—plants as different as cactus and columbine! Most useful for cooking is honey from clover or alfalfa. These are mild and will not distract attention from the foods they are used to sweeten.

Because it has the tendency to draw water to itself, foods made with honey may become sticky or runny. Use only enough to enhance the natural sweetness of the fruit without overpowering the flavor.

One tablespoon honey contains 17.3 grams sugar while one tablespoon refined sugar contains only 11.9 grams. This means that honey is forty-five percent more concentrated than table sugar! Since the sweetening power of honey is greater than sugar, a little does a lot. *Honey should not be used by diabetics and hypoglycemics.* While a natural sugar, it can still overload the pancreas. Recipes in this section cannot be used by anyone with either of these metabolic problems. On the basis of some recent research, some physicians recommend that honey not be consumed by infants less than one year of age because of the risk of infant botulism.

Fruits canned without added sugar tend to lose color: cherries or strawberries can fade almost to white after a year's storage. With honey, colors stay true and there is no more fading than with refined sugar canning. All foods canned with honey should be processed by water bath or pressure cooker. Honey-canned fruit will be sweeter than when preserved using only fruit juice, and honey-sweetened fruits, jams, and preserves will better suit a sugar-lover's taste. Honey isn't cheap, but it takes so little to sweeten, using these recipes, that it ends up costing less than fruit juice.

Fruit flavors are delicate; be sure to taste the fruit-honey combination you plan to use before making a whole batch. To can fruit with honey syrup, follow directions for selecting and preparing fruit (see Index), and make syrup according to the following directions.

How to Make Honey-Sweetened Syrup

Light Syrup: 2 tablespoons honey plus 1½ to 2 teaspoons lemon juice (larger amount for sweet fruit) plus boiled water equals 1 cup syrup

Medium Syrup: 3 tablespoons honey plus 2 to 3 teaspoons lemon juice plus boiled water equals 1 cup syrup

Plan to add a few fruit pits to the fruit when using honey. This will add an almond-like taste which will blend well and help disguise the honey flavor. Do not use more honey than called for or the fruit flavor will be lost.

Process and pack fruit as directed in previous section (Preserving with Fruit Juice Sweetening–see Index). You do not have to process honey-sweetened fruit when doing hot pack canning; just be sure jars and lids are sterile. The honey will prevent bacterial growth.

Applesauce with Honey

Apples 6 cups quartered with stem and blossom end removed
Water 1¼ cups
Lemon juice 3 tablespoons
Honey ⅓ cup
Lemon rind ⅓ teaspoon grated (optional)
Cinnamon ¾ teaspoon (optional)
Salt dash (optional)

Place apples and water in deep nonaluminum kettle. Cover and cook until very soft. Remove from heat and put through food mill. Return pureed material to kettle. Add remaining ingredients and reheat to boiling. Simmer for 5 minutes. Pour into hot, sterile jars, leaving ¾ inch at top. Cap with hot, sterile lids. If any jars fail to seal, process in boiling water bath for 10 minutes after water has returned to boiling, or in pressure cooker for 10 minutes at 5 pounds pressure. If any still fail to seal, refrigerate and use within a few days. Makes 6 cups.

Nutritional value: ½ cup contains 64 Calories. *This should not be used by diabetics or hypoglycemics.* ½ cup contains less than 2 milligrams sodium if no salt is used.

Jam and Jelly

Honey can precipitate pectin just as refined sugar does, provided enough is present. To convert other recipes, substitute honey at the rate of one-third the volume of sugar called for. Always use liquid (not powdered) pectin when cooking with honey; it mixes readily and eliminates delay. Lemon juice is usually added to cut the honey taste (one tablespoon lemon juice or more for each one-fourth cup honey). With too little honey, regular pectin will not jell and glycerine must then be added (one-half to one tablespoon glycerine for each cup cooked fruit mixture). The amount of acid present also affects the jell; with too much acid, pectin will not jell, either.

While it can be tricky to get honey jams and jellies to come out just right, when they do, they are delightful. Instead of making jelly or jam (other than with the tested recipes provided), why not omit pectin entirely and make preserves with honey. That way you don't have to worry about the pectin jelling and whether or not to use glycerine to help the jell.

The recipes that follow are samples of the good things that can be made with honey. To experiment with other recipes, just use the same amount of fruit/juice and pectin as usual, but add honey equal to one-third the amount of sugar. Make a small batch in case it doesn't thicken as you'd like. If it is too thin, reheat and add glycerine (2 teaspoons per cup jam) or unflavored gelatin (one tablespoon per four cups jam/jelly). Either will thicken satisfactorily.

While I don't recommend it, jams made with honey can be preserved with paraffin, just as jams made with sugar. Be sure jars and utensils are sterile (see "How to Sterilize Equipment"). Immediately cover jelly/jam with hot melted wax before it has a chance to gather bacteria from the air. (The high sugar content normally acts as a bacteria inhibitor.) But if you want to be very sure and safe, cover with hot sealing lids and process in boiling water bath for five to ten minutes after water has returned to boiling, or in pressure cooker for five minutes at five pounds pressure. When paraffin is cool, cover with lids or make covers from heavy paper or foil so dust won't gather on top of the wax. Store as recommended for all jam/jelly/preserves in a cool, dark cupboard.

Basic Jam Recipe
(with Honey and Regular Pectin)

Fresh fruit   2 cups pitted and chopped
Water   ¼ cup
Lemon juice   2 tablespoons
Honey   ½ cup
Lemon rind   ½ teaspoon (optional)
Liquid pectin (regular)   ½ cup
Salt   dash (optional)
Spices (cinnamon, nutmeg, cloves, etc.)   ½ to 1 teaspoon (optional)
Gelatin   1 tablespoon (1 envelope) (optional)

Place fruit, water, juice, honey, and lemon rind in deep nonaluminum pan. Cook until fruit is soft, mashing for more uniform texture. Add pectin, return to heat, and bring to a rolling boil for 1 minute. Remove from heat, skim and add spices. If using gelatin, sprinkle over hot mixture, stirring well. Pour immediately into clean, hot jars, leaving ¾ inch at top.

Cap with hot lids (jars and lids must be sterilized before using if jam is not to be processed in water bath or pressure cooker) or use hot paraffin (two layers) to completely seal. If any jars fail to seal, process in boiling water bath for 10 minutes after water returns to boiling, or in pressure cooker for 10 minutes at 5 pounds pressure. Makes 3 cups.

Nutritional value: Depending upon fruit used, 1 tablespoon contains from 12 to 40 Calories. *This should not be used by diabetics or hypoglycemics.* If no salt is added, 1 tablespoon contains less than 1 milligram sodium.

Berry Jam with Honey

Whole berries   2 cups
Water   ¼ cup
Lemon juice   2 tablespoons
Honey   ½ cup
Salt   dash (optional)
Liquid pectin (regular)   ½ cup
Gelatin   1 tablespoon (1 envelope) (optional)

Place berries, water, lemon juice, honey, and salt in deep nonaluminum saucepan. Cook until berries are soft, mashing them for more uniform texture, if desired. Add pectin, return to heat, and bring to a rolling boil. If using gelatin, sprinkle over hot mixture, stirring well. Pour immediately into clean, hot jars, leaving ¾ inch at top. Cap with hot lids (jars and lids must be sterilized before using if jam is not to be processed in water bath or pressure cooker) or immediately pour 2 layers of melted paraffin over the jam to completely seal. If using lids, process in boiling water bath for 10 minutes after water returns to boiling, or in pressure cooker for 10 minutes at 5 pounds pressure. Makes 3 cups.
Note: If made with strawberries, reduce water to 2 tablespoons.

Nutritional value: 1 tablespoon contains 12 Calories (P0,F0,C3). *This should not be used by diabetics or hypoglycemics.* If no salt is added, 1 tablespoon contains less than 1 milligram sodium.

Rhubarb-Strawberry Jam with Honey

Rhubarb   6 cups cut into ½ inch pieces
Water   1 cup
Strawberries   3 cups hulled and halved
Lemon juice   3 tablespoons
Salt   dash (optional)
Honey   1½ cups
Liquid pectin (regular)   6 ounces (1 package)

Place rhubarb and water in deep nonaluminum kettle. Bring to a boil, turn down heat, cover, and cook until rhubarb is almost soft. Add berries, lemon juice, and salt and recover and cook until fruit is very soft. Add honey and bring to a boil. Stir in pectin and return to heat, bringing to a rolling boil for 1 minute. Skim and immediately pour into clean, hot jars, leaving ¾ inch at top. Cap with hot lids (jars and lids must be sterilized before using if jam is not to be processed in water bath or pressure cooker) or cover with 2 layers of hot paraffin. If lids fail to seal, process in boiling water bath for 10 minutes after water returns to boiling, or in pressure cooker for 10 minutes at 5 pounds pressure. Makes 9½ to 10 cups.

Nutritional value: 1 tablespoon contains 12 Calories. *This should not be used by diabetics or hypoglycemics.* If no salt is added, 3 tablespoons contain 1 milligram sodium.

Tomato Jam with Honey

Tomatoes   2 pounds, skinned, chopped, with juice
Lemons   1⅓ juiced, rind ground or finely chopped
Honey   ½ cup
Liquid pectin (regular)   ½ cup
Ginger   ½ teaspoon (optional)
Mace   ½ teaspoon (optional)
Salt   dash (optional)

Combine tomatoes, lemon rind and juice, and honey in deep nonaluminum pan. Simmer until lemon pieces are tender and jam is fairly thick. Add pectin and reheat to rolling boil. Boil for 1 minute. Add spices, stir, and pour into clean, hot jars, leaving ¾ inch at top. Cap with hot lids. Process in boiling water bath for 10 minutes after water returns to boiling, or in pressure cooker for 10 minutes at 10 pounds pressure. If any jars do not seal, use immediately. Makes 5 cups.
Variation: To make this as a relish, add ¼ cup vinegar to the tomato-

lemon mixture and omit the suggested seasonings, replacing with ¾ to 1 teaspoon ground allspice.

Nutritional value: 1 tablespoon contains 12 Calories (P0,F0,C2½). *This should not be used by diabetics or hypoglycemics.* If no salt is added, 2 tablespoons equal 1 milligram sodium.

Mother's Carrot Jam or Preserves with Honey

Carrots 1½ cups sliced
Honey ½ cup
Water ¾ cup
Large lemon 1, with juice and ½ the rind, finely chopped
Walnuts or pecans ¼ cup chopped
Low methoxy pectin solution ¼ cup (optional)
Calcium solution 1¼ teaspoons (optional)

Peel or scrape carrots, slice, and place in saucepan. Cover with water and simmer until tender. Drain, discarding water. (Or save it for soup; It is rich in vitamins and minerals.) Mash carrots and measure to be sure you have 1½ cups. Return to saucepan and add honey, water, lemon juice, and lemon rind. Cook for 5 minutes over low heat. Add nuts.

If you continue cooking, volume will be reduced and a preserve will be the result. Or add pectin, bring to a boil, add calcium, and stir. Pour into sterile, hot jars, leaving ¾ inch at top. Cover jars with 2 layers of hot paraffin or use hot, sterile lids screwed down tightly, and allow to stand. If any jar fails to seal, process in boiling water bath for 10 minutes after water returns to boiling, or in pressure cooker for 10 minutes at 5 pounds pressure. Makes 2½ cups.*
* If pectin is not used, volume will be reduced to about 1½ cups.

Nutritional value: With pectin, 2 tablespoons contain 33 Calories (P1,F1,C5). Without pectin, 2 tablespoons contain 50 Calories (P1,F1,C7). *This should not be used by diabetics or hypoglycemics.* If no salt is added, 2 tablespoons contain 3 milligrams sodium.

Basic Jelly Recipe with Honey and Regular Pectin

Fruit juice   2 cups
Lemon juice   1½ to 2 tablespoons
Honey   ½ cup
Salt   dash (optional)
Liquid pectin (regular)   2 ounces (⅓ package)
Gelatin   1 tablespoon (1 envelope) (optional)

Place juices, honey, and salt in saucepan. Bring to a boil. Add pectin and gelatin, stir, and return to a rolling boil for 1 minute. Pour immediately into hot, sterile jars, leaving ¾ inch at top. Cap with hot, sterile lids screwed down tightly, or top jelly with 2 layers of melted paraffin. If using lids and they fail to seal, process in boiling water bath for 10 minutes after water returns to boiling, or in pressure cooker for 10 minutes at 5 pounds pressure. Makes 2½ cups.

Nutritional value: 1 tablespoon contains from 30 to 40 Calories depending upon juice used. *This should not be used by diabetics or hypoglycemics.* If no salt is used, 1 tablespoon contains less than 1 milligram sodium.

Grape Jelly with Honey

Concord grape juice   3 cups or
    Concord grape juice   2 cups and
    White grape juice   1 cup
Lemon juice   1½ tablespoons
Honey   ½ cup
Salt   dash (optional)
Liquid pectin (regular)   2 ounces (⅓ package)
Gelatin   1 tablespoon (1 envelope) (optional)

Simmer grape juice down to 2 cups, then add lemon juice, honey, and salt. Bring to a boil and stir in pectin and gelatin, bring to a rolling boil for 1 minute. Remove from heat and pour immediately into hot, sterile jars, leaving ¾ inch at top. Cap with hot, sterile lids. Process jars that do not seal for 10 minutes after water has returned to boiling, or in pressure cooker for 10 minutes at 5 pounds pressure. If jar still does not seal, refrigerate and use within next 10 days. Makes 2½ cups.
Variation: Use white grape juice only and add ¾ to 1 teaspoon dried

marjoram or thyme to the juice as you simmer it down. Strain to remove herbs and continue as directed.

Nutritional value: 1 tablespoon contains 32 Calories (P0,F0,C8). *This should not be used by diabetics or hypoglycemics.* If no salt is added, 4 tablespoons contain less than 1 milligram sodium.

Honey-Lemon Jelly

Lemon rind   1 teaspoon grated (optional)
Honey   1¼ cups
Water   ¾ cup
Lemon juice   2 tablespoons
Ginger   1 teaspoon (optional)
Liquid pectin (regular)   2 ounces (⅓ package)

If using lemon rind, simmer with honey and water for 10 minutes; allow to stand for 20 minutes to emphasize the lemon flavor. Combine honey, water, lemon juice, and lemon rind in deep nonaluminum saucepan. Bring to a boil. Add ginger and pectin, return to heat, and bring to a rolling boil for 1 minute. Pour into hot, sterile jars, leaving ¾ inch at top. Cap with hot, sterile lids. Process jars that do not seal in boiling water bath for 10 minutes after water has returned to boiling, or in pressure cooker for 10 minutes at 5 pounds pressure. If any jar still fails to seal, refrigerate and use within 10 days. Makes 2¼ cups.

Nutritional value: 1 tablespoon contains 40 Calories (P0,F0,C10). *This should not be used by diabetics or hypoglycemics.* If no salt is added, 1 tablespoon contains less than 1 milligram sodium.

Preserves

Basic Preserves with Honey

Fresh fruit   6 cups pitted and chopped
Other fruit   1 cup pitted or seeded and chopped
Water   ½ cup
Honey   ¾ to 1 cup
Lemon juice   3 tablespoons
Spices (cinnamon, nutmeg, cloves, ginger, etc.)   (optional)
Salt   dash (optional)

Combine fruit, water, honey, and juice in large nonaluminum kettle. Bring to a boil, then simmer until thickened, adding spices toward end of cooking time. Skim and pour into sterile jars, leaving ¾ inch at top. Cap with sterile lids. If any jar fails to seal, process in boiling water bath for 10 minutes after water returns to boiling, or in pressure cooker for 10 minutes at 5 pounds pressure, or cover with 2 layers melted paraffin. Makes 6 cups.

Nutritional value: 1 tablespoon contains from 28 to 40 Calories, depending upon fruits used. *This should not be used by diabetics or hypoglycemics.* If no salt is added, 1 tablespoon contains less than 1 milligram sodium.

Apricot-Orange Butter with Honey

Fresh apricots   6 cups pitted or
    Dried apricots   1½ pounds (6 cups after soaking)
Water   ½ cup
Concentrated orange juice   ½ cup
Honey   ¼ cup for each cup puree
Cinnamon   1 teaspoon
Nutmeg   ½ teaspoon
Ginger   ¼ teaspoon (optional)
Salt   dash (optional)

If using dried apricots, soak overnight in water and juice plus enough additional water to cover. In the morning, place in deep nonaluminum kettle and simmer until tender. Puree in food mill or blender, sieving afterward to remove pieces (reblend and add to rest). Measure puree volume and add ¼ cup honey for each cup puree. Add spices, and salt, and continue to simmer until thick, stirring often to prevent sticking.

Skim and pour immediately into hot, sterile jars. Leave ¾ inch at top of jar and cap with hot, sterile lids or cover with 2 layers melted paraffin to completely seal. If any jars fail to seal, process in boiling water bath for 10 minutes after water returns to boiling, or in pressure cooker for 10 minutes after it has reached 5 pounds pressure. Makes 5 cups.

Nutritional value: 1 tablespoon contains 42 Calories (P½,F0,C10). *This should not be used by diabetics or hypoglycemics.* If no salt is added, 2 tablespoons contain 1 milligram sodium.

Blueberry-Pineapple Preserves with Honey

Blueberries 4 cups, washed, stems removed
Water 2 tablespoons
Lemon juice 3 tablespoons
Crushed pineapple 2 cups (in own juice)
Honey 1½ cups
Lemon rind 1 tablespoon grated
Salt dash (optional)
Cinnamon 1½ teaspoons (optional)

Place berries in deep nonaluminum kettle. Add water and juice. Cook until tender, mashing to break up whole berries. Add pineapple, honey, rind, salt, and cinnamon. Cook until thick. Skim and pack immediately in hot, sterile jars, leaving ¾ inch at top. Cap with hot, sterile lids. If any jars fail to seal, process for 10 minutes in boiling water bath, or in pressure cooker for 10 minutes at 5 pounds pressure. Makes 4 cups.

Nutritional value: 1 tablespoon contains 36 Calories (P0,F0,C9). *This should not be used by diabetics or hypoglycemics.* If no salt is added, 1 tablespoon contains less than 1 milligram sodium.

Purple Plum Conserve with Honey

Purple plums, prune-type   6 cups chopped, pitted
Medium orange   1, seeded, chopped, including peel
Medium lemon   1, seeded, chopped, including peel
Water   ¾ cup
Honey   1½ cups
Seedless raisins   2 cups
Salt   dash (optional)
Pecans or walnuts   ¾ cup chopped

Place plums, orange, lemon, and water in a deep nonaluminum kettle. Cover and simmer for 25 minutes. Add honey, raisins, and salt, and continue to cook until thick. Add nuts, mix well, skim, pack immediately into hot, sterile jars, leaving ¾ inch at top. Cap with sterile lids or cover with 2 layers melted paraffin to completely seal. If any jars fail to seal, process in boiling water bath for 10 minutes after water returns to boiling, or in pressure cooker for 10 minutes at 5 pounds pressure. Makes 9½ cups.

Nutritional value: 1 tablespoon contains 25 Calories (P0,F½,C5). *This should not be used by diabetics or hypoglycemics.* If no salt is added, 1 tablespoon contains less than 1 milligram sodium.

Basic Frozen Preserves with Honey

Fruit   4 cups chopped or sliced, including juice
Lemon juice   3 tablespoons
Water   ¼ cup (may omit if fruit is juicy)
Orange or lemon rind   1 teaspoon to 1 tablespoon grated
Honey   1½ to 2 cups
Salt   dash (optional)
Spices (cinnamon, nutmeg, cloves, ginger, etc.)   to taste (optional)

Place fruit, juice, and water in deep nonaluminum kettle. Bring to a boil and simmer until fruit is tender. Add remaining ingredients and return to heat. Simmer until thickened. Use spices lightly and taste after a few minutes; add more if desired. Skim and pack immediately into hot, sterile jars, leaving ¾ inch at top. Cap with sterile lids and set aside to cool to room temperature. When cool, sharp freeze, moving to main freezer for storage. Makes 5 cups.

Nutritional value: 1 tablespoon contains from 28 to 40 Calories depending upon fruit used (P0,F0,C7-10). *This should not be used by diabetics or hypoglycemics.* If no salt is added, 1 tablespoon contains less than 1 milligram sodium.

Frozen Strawberry Preserves with Honey

Strawberries 4 cups washed and hulled
Lemon juice 3 tablespoons
Water ¼ cup
Honey 1½ cups
Salt dash (optional)
Lemon rind ½ teaspoon grated (optional)

Place berries, lemon juice, and water in saucepan; cover and simmer until tender. (Mash berries to release more juice if desired.) Add honey and salt and continue to cook until thick. Taste, add lemon rind, if desired, and heat 1 minute longer. Skim and pour immediately into hot, sterile jars, leaving ¾ inch at top. Cap with sterile lids. Set aside to cool to room temperature. When cool, sharp freeze, moving to main freezer section for storage. Makes 4½ cups.

Nutritional value: 1½ tablespoons contain 40 Calories (P0,F0,C10). *This should not be used by diabetics or hypoglycemics.* If no salt is added, 2 tablespoons contain 1 milligram sodium.

Meatless Mincemeat

Meatless Mincemeat with Honey

Follow recipe for Basic Sugarless Vegetarian Mincemeat (see Index), but instead of date sugar, substitute ¼ to ½ cup honey. If the same volume honey as date sugar is used, the nutritional value does not change significantly. If the honey is increased to ½ cup, the values are:

Regular date sugar recipe, 116 Calories per ¼ cup

With ¼ cup honey substituted for date sugar, 124 Calories per ¼ cup

With ½ cup honey substituted for date sugar, 144 Calories per ¼ cup

Sodium content is not altered by substituting honey for date sugar. ¼ cup contains 7 milligrams sodium.

Variation: To make Green Tomato Mincemeat with Honey, follow recipe for Green Tomato Mincemeat (see Index), but omit date sugar and substitute ½ cup honey.

Nutritional value: ¼ cup contains 90 Calories. ¼ cup contains 5 milligrams sodium. *Diabetics or hypoglycemics should not use these recipes with honey.*

Pickles, Relishes, and Seasoning Sauces

Pickle, relish, and sauce recipes can be made with honey instead of sugar, but the amount used is half or less. It is hard to keep honey flavor from intruding, so in some recipes a degree of sweetness has been sacrificed to avoid this. Pickle and relish recipes in the section using fruit juices for sweetening (see Index) can be made with honey instead. Omit fruit juice and use half as much honey as the recipe calls for with concentrated fruit juice, or one-eighth as much using regular fruit juice. Make a small trial batch to be sure the sweetness is right. Pickles made with honey will keep without final processing in water bath or pressure cooker, but jars must be well sealed. Any that do not seal must be processed as indicated.

Pickled Beets with Honey

Tiny beets   12 cups
Whole allspice   1 teaspoon
Whole cloves   ½ teaspoon
Cinnamon sticks   2, broken into 4 pieces
Lemon juice   1½ tablespoons
Honey   1 cup
Cider vinegar   2 cups
Water   2 cups plus water to cook beets

Wash beets, and cut off tops, leaving at least 1 inch to prevent bleeding. Cover with water and cook until tender. Drain and cool sufficiently to handle easily. Remove skin and trim tops and roots uniformly. If any are too large, slice and pack separately. Make a bag for spices and place in deep saucepan along with lemon juice, honey, vinegar, and 2 cups of water. Bring to a boil, add beets, and cook for 10 minutes. Remove spice bag and pack beets immediately into hot, clean jars, leaving 1 inch at top. Cover with hot lids and process in boiling water bath for 30 minutes after water returns to boiling, or in pressure cooker for 25 minutes at 10 pounds pressure. Makes 3 quarts.

Nutritional value: ¼ cup contains 28 Calories (P0,F0,C7). *This should not be used by diabetics or hypoglycemics.* If fresh beets are used, ¼ cup contains 21 milligrams sodium.

Corn Relish with Honey

Whole kernel corn 4 cups (cut from ears or frozen)
Green cabbage 1¼ cups chopped
Medium white onions 3, chopped
Green peppers 2, seeded, stems removed
Small red peppers (hot or sweet) 2, seeded, stems removed
Pimento 3 tablespoons minced
Celery seed ⅔ teaspoon
Mustard seed ⅔ teaspoon
Cider vinegar 2½ cups
Salt or salt substitute 1 tablespoon
Honey ½ cup*

Place corn in large nonaluminum kettle. Grind other vegetables in meat grinder using coarse blade. Add with remaining ingredients to corn and bring to a boil. Turn down heat and simmer for 35 minutes. Skim and pack immediately into clean, hot jars, leaving 1 inch at top. Cap with hot lids and process in boiling water bath for 20 minutes after water returns to boiling, or in pressure cooker for 20 minutes at 10 pounds pressure. Makes 8½ to 9 cups.

* A diabetic version of this recipe could be made by omitting honey and using ¾ cup concentrated apple juice and 2 tablespoons lemon juice. In that case, 2 tablespoons contain 18 Calories (P0,F0,C4½). ¼ cup equals 1 diabetic fruit exchange. Sodium is unchanged.

Nutritional value: 2 tablespoons contain 20 Calories (P0,F0,C5). If fresh corn is used and no salt is added, 2 tablespoons contain 4 milligrams sodium. If frozen corn is used, 2 tablespoons contain about 12 milligrams sodium.

Indian Chutney with Honey

Large, ripe tomatoes 5
Large onions 3, peeled and chopped
Green pepper 1, seeded and chopped
Hot or sweet red pepper 1, seeded
Large tart apples 4, seeded and cored
Seedless raisins ¾ cup
Honey ⅓ cup*
Cider vinegar 1⅓ cups
Salt or salt substitute 1½ teaspoons
Curry powder 1 teaspoon

Grind all fruits and vegetables in meat grinder using medium blade. Place in deep nonaluminum kettle and add honey, vinegar, salt, and curry. Simmer until thickened, about 1 hour. Skim and pour into hot, sterile jars, leaving 1 inch at top. Cap with hot, sterile lids. Process in boiling water bath for 20 minutes after water returns to boiling, or in pressure cooker for 20 minutes at 10 pounds pressure. Makes 8 cups.
* A diabetic version of this recipe could be made by omitting honey and substituting ½ cup concentrated apple juice and 2 tablespoons lemon juice. 2 tablespoons would contain 20 Calories (P0,F0,C5). In that case, ¼ cup equals 1 diabetic fruit exchange. Sodium is unchanged.

Nutritional value: 2 tablespoons contain 20 Calories (P0,F0,C5). If no salt is added, 2 tablespoons contain 2 milligrams sodium.

Sweet Hot Pepper Relish with Honey

Large red peppers 6, seeded and chopped
Large green peppers 6, seeded and chopped
Medium onions 6, peeled and chopped
Salt or salt substitute 2 tablespoons
Pickling vinegar 1½ cups
Lemon juice 2 tablespoons
Cayenne pepper ½ teaspoon
Honey ½ to ¾ cup
Tabasco sauce dash (optional)

Grind vegetables in meat grinder using medium-coarse blade. Mix with salt and let stand 4 hours or overnight. Drain and discard liquid. Put drained vegetables in large nonaluminum kettle and add remaining ingredients. Cook over low heat until thickened, ¾ hour or more. Taste, add more cayenne (or Tabasco sauce) if desired. Pour into hot, clean jars, leaving 1 inch at top. Cap with hot lids and process in boiling water bath for 10 minutes (15 minutes for quart jars) after water has returned to boiling, or in pressure cooker for 10 minutes at 10 pounds pressure. Makes 7 cups.

Nutritional value: 1 tablespoon contains 12 Calories (P0,F0,C3). If the larger amount of honey is used, 1 tablespoon contains 14 Calories (P0,F0,C3½). *This should not be used by diabetics or hypoglycemics.* If no salt substitute is used, 1 tablespoon contains less than 3 milligrams sodium.

Sweet Tomato Pickles with Honey

Green or unripe tomatoes   8 cups
Large onions   2, peeled and sliced
Large apple   1, peeled, cored, and chopped
Salt or salt substitute   ¼ cup
Cider vinegar   1 cup
Honey   ½ cup
Cloves   1½ teaspoons
Dry mustard   1½ teaspoons
Cinnamon   1½ teaspoons
Cayenne pepper   ⅛ teaspoon

Peel and slice tomatoes, slice onions and apple, and place all in large bowl. Add salt, mix, and let stand at least 12 hours. Drain and discard liquid. Add vinegar and simmer for 45 minutes. Add remaining ingredients and cook 20 to 30 minutes longer until thick. Skim and pack into hot, clean jars, leaving 1 inch at top. Cover with hot lids and process in boiling water bath for 10 minutes after water has returned to boiling, or in pressure cooker for 10 minutes at 10 pounds pressure. Makes 8 cups.

Nutritional value: 1 tablespoon contains 12 Calories (P0,F0,C3). *This should not be used by diabetics or hypoglycemics.* If salt substitute is used, 1 tablespoon contains less than 1 milligram sodium.

Fruit Relish with Honey

Unsweetened applesauce (see Index)   2 cups
Honey   1 to 1½ teaspoons
Lemon juice   1½ tablespoons
Prepared horseradish   2 tablespoons
Lemon rind   ¼ teaspoon grated (optional)
Salt   dash (optional)

Place applesauce in mixing bowl and add smaller amount of honey and remaining ingredients. Mix well. Taste. Add remaining honey if desired. Pack into sterile jars, leaving 1 inch at top. Cover with sterile lids. Cool and freeze or process in boiling water bath for 10 minutes after water has returned to boiling, or in pressure cooker for 10 minutes at 5 pounds pressure. Makes 2 cups.

Nutritional value: 1 tablespoon contains 12 Calories (P0,F0,C3). *This should not be used by diabetics or hypoglycemics.* If no salt is added, 1 tablespoon contains 1 milligram sodium.

Barbecue Sauce with Honey

Tomato puree   2 cups or
   Tomato paste   1 cup and
   Water   1 cup
Honey   1 tablespoon or more*
Onion powder   ½ teaspoon
Allspice   ⅛ teaspoon
Garlic powder   ⅛ teaspoon
Cider vinegar   ½ cup
Worcestershire sauce   ½ teaspoon

Mix all ingredients and stir well. Heat to boiling, then pack into sterile jars, leaving 1 inch at top. Cover with sterile lids. Set aside to cool before freezing, or process in boiling water bath for 15 minutes after water has returned to boiling, or in pressure cooker for 15 minutes at 10 pounds pressure. Makes 2½ cups.
* This can be made into a diabetic recipe by omitting honey and substituting 2 tablespoons concentrated apple juice. ½ cup would contain 36 Calories (P2,F0,C9). ½ cup would equal ½ diabetic bread exchange or 1 diabetic fruit exchange.
Variation: For hot barbecue sauce, add ½ teaspoon tabasco sauce and ¼ to ½ teaspoon cayenne pepper.

Nutritional value: ½ cup contains 40 Calories (P2,F0,C8). If no salt is added and salt-free puree is used, 2 tablespoons sauce will contain 14 milligrams sodium.

Tomato Catsup with Honey

Ripe tomatoes or whole canned, drained   8 cups, peeled and quartered
Medium onions   2, peeled and chopped
Large green pepper   1, seeded and chopped
Small garlic cloves   4, minced
Large celery stalks   2, diced
Cider vinegar   1 cup
Honey   ½ cup*
Cloves   ½ teaspoon
Dry mustard   1 teaspoon
Mace   ½ teaspoon
Allspice   1 teaspoon
Tabasco sauce   ¼ teaspoon (optional)
Lemon juice   2 tablespoons
Salt or salt substitute   1 tablespoon
Black pepper   ½ teaspoon

Combine all ingredients in large nonaluminum kettle. Cook slowly over low heat until vegetables are very soft, being careful to prevent mixture from boiling. Remove from heat and put through food mill. Return to heat and bring to boil. Pour into sterile jars, leaving 1 inch at the top. Cap with sterile lids and process in boiling water bath for 15 minutes after water has returned to boiling, or in pressure cooker for 15 minutes at 10 pounds pressure. Makes 4 pints.
* This can be made into a diabetic recipe by omitting honey, substituting ¾ cup concentrated apple juice and increasing lemon juice to 4 tablespoons. In that case, 1 tablespoon contains 12 Calories (P0,F0,C3). 4 tablespoons equal 1 diabetic fruit exchange, 2 tablespoons equal 1 vegetable exchange.

Nutritional value: 1 tablespoon contains 16 Calories (P0,F0,C4). If made with honey, *this should not be used by diabetics or hypoglycemics.* If fresh tomatoes are used and no salt is added, 1 tablespoon contains 1 milligram sodium.

Winter Recipes Using Honey

All-year-round recipes made from nonseasonal fruits and vegetables follow. Many of the recipes presented in preceding sections can also be made during the winter or off-season: Try "Applesauce with Honey," "Mincemeat," "Fruit Relish" (see Index), or others adaptable to ingredients available during winter months.

Apricot-Pineapple Jam with Honey

Dried apricots   1 pound
Water
Crushed pineapple   2 cups (in own juice)
Lemon   ¼, seeded and chopped
Lemon juice   ¼ cup
Honey   ¾ cup
Salt   dash (optional)

Soak apricots overnight in warm water (just enough to cover). In morning, place in deep nonaluminum kettle, add pineapple, lemon, and juice. (Add more water for cooking if all was absorbed into dried fruit.) Cook slowly until fruit is tender and mixture thickened. Add honey and cook for 3 minutes longer, stirring to prevent sticking. Remove from heat, skim and pour into hot, sterile jars, leaving ¾ inch at top. Cap with hot lids. If any jar fails to seal, process in boiling water bath for 10 minutes after water returns to boiling, or in pressure cooker for 10 minutes at 5 pounds pressure. If any still fail to seal, refrigerate and use within 10 days. Makes 5 cups.

Nutritional value: 1 tablespoon contains 20 Calories. *This should not be used by diabetics or hypoglycemics.* If no salt is used, 1 tablespoon contains less than 1 milligram sodium.

Frozen Blueberry-Pineapple Preserves with Honey

Frozen blueberries   4 cups
Crushed pineapple   2 cups (in own juice)
Water   ¼ cup
Lemon juice   3 tablespoons
Lemon rind   2 teaspoons grated
Honey   1½ cups
Cinnamon or nutmeg   ½ teaspoon
Unflavored gelatin   1 tablespoon (1 envelope)
Salt   dash (optional)

Place berries, pineapple, water, lemon juice, and lemon rind in deep nonaluminum kettle. Cook slowly until berries are tender. Remove from heat, add honey, spices, gelatin, and salt; return to heat, and cook until thick. Skim and pour into hot, sterile jars, leaving ¾ inch at top. Cap with hot, sterile lids. To freeze, allow to stand until room temperature before putting into sharp freeze section of freezer; otherwise check jars to be sure lids have sealed. If any fail to seal, process in boiling water bath for 10 minutes after water returns to boiling, or 10 minutes in pressure cooker at 5 pounds pressure. If any still fail to seal, refrigerate and use within 10 days. Makes 4 cups.

Nutritional value: 1 tablespoon contains 36 Calories. *This should not be used by diabetics or hypoglycemics.* If no salt is added, 1 tablespoon contains less than 1 milligram sodium.

Prune Conserve with Honey

Medium prunes   1 pound, pitted
Seedless raisins   1 cup
Water   2 cups
Crushed pineapple   1 cup (in own juice)
Medium orange   1, with juice and chopped rind
Medium lemon   ½, with juice and chopped rind
Honey   ½ cup
Walnuts or pecans   ½ cup chopped
Lemon rind   1 teaspoon grated (optional)
Salt   dash (optional)

Soak prunes and raisins overnight in the water with any juices from the orange and lemon. In the morning, place in deep nonaluminum saucepan with all other ingredients except nuts. Simmer until thick, stirring often to prevent sticking. When thick, add nuts, heat 1 minute more. Skim and pack immediately in hot, sterile jars, leaving ¾ inch at top. Cap with hot, sterile lids. If any jar fails to seal, process in boiling water bath for 10 minutes after water returns to boiling, or in pressure cooker for 10 minutes at 5 pounds pressure. Makes 7 cups.

Nutritional value: 2 tablespoons contain 61 Calories (P0,F1,C13). *This should not be used by diabetics or hypoglycemics.* If no salt is added, 2 tablespoons contain 2 milligrams sodium.

Winter Pear Jam with Honey

Ripe winter pears   3 pounds, peeled and cored
Medium orange   1, seeded
Medium lemon   1, seeded
Crushed pineapple   1 cup (in own juice)
Honey   ¾ cup
Fresh ginger root   1 inch, peeled and thinly sliced
Whole cloves   6
Cinnamon sticks   2, broken into 3 pieces
Salt   dash (optional)

Using coarse blade of meat grinder, grind fruits. Place in deep nonaluminum kettle, adding pineapple and juice. Add remaining ingredients and simmer until fruit is tender and mixture thick. Skim and pour into hot, sterile jars, leaving ¾ inch at top. Cap with hot, sterile lids and check for seal after they have cooled. If any jars fail to seal, process in boiling water bath for 10 minutes after water has returned to boiling, or in pressure cooker for 10 minutes at 5 pounds pressure. If any still fail to seal, refrigerate and use within 10 days. Makes 3 pints.

Nutritional value: 1 tablespoon contains 20 Calories. *This should not be used by diabetics or hypoglycemics.* 1 tablespoon contains 2 milligrams sodium.

Winter Marmalade with Honey

Carrots   3 large bunches (approximately 4 pounds)
Water
Large grapefruit   1
Large lemons   2
Large orange   1
Large tangerines   2
Honey   4 cups

Peel or scrape carrots, cover with water, and cook until tender. Drain and discard water (or save to use; it is rich in vitamins and minerals). Mash to make uniform pieces. Squeeze juice from fruit, add to carrots. Cut rinds into chunks, cover with water, and cook for 15 minutes. Drain and add liquid to carrots. Chop rinds into very narrow strips. Add to carrots, along with honey. Refrigerate overnight. Boil in deep nonaluminum pan until thick. Remove from heat, skim and pack immediately into hot, sterile jars, leaving ¾ inch at top. Cap with sterile lids or seal with 2 layers melted paraffin. If jars fail to seal, process in boiling water bath for 10 minutes after water has returned to boiling, or in pressure cooker for 10 minutes at 5 pounds pressure. Makes 10 cups.

Nutritional value: 1 tablespoon contains 34 Calories (P0,F0,C8½). *This should not be used by diabetics or hypoglycemics.* 1 tablespoon contains 16 milligrams sodium.

Preserved Orange Slices with Honey

Large, thin-skinned oranges   6
Lemon slices   2, seeded and diced
Water   1 quart (approximately)
Lemon juice   ¼ cup
Honey   1 cup

Wash and dry oranges. Cut off and discard ends, then cut about 3 slices per inch, including rind, but removing seeds. Place in deep nonaluminum saucepan, adding lemon and juice plus enough water to cover. Cover pan and simmer until rind is tender and translucent. Add honey and simmer 5 minutes more. Place slices in wide mouth hot, clean jars, leaving 1 inch at top. Cover with hot liquid. Cap with hot lids. Process in boiling water bath for 10 minutes after water returns to boiling, or in pressure cooker for 10 minutes at 5 pounds pressure. Makes 6 cups.

Nutritional value: 2 slices contain 64 Calories. *This should not be used by diabetics or hypoglycemics.* 2 slices contain less than 1 milligram sodium.

Winter Indian Chutney with Honey

Canned tomatoes, canned with juice 4 cups, chopped, with juice
Large onions 3, peeled
Large green pepper 1, seeded
Dried hot red pepper 1½ to 2 tablespoons
Large tart apples 4, seeded and cored
Seedless raisins ⅞ cup
Honey ⅓ cup
Cider vinegar 1⅓ cups
Salt or salt substitute 1½ teaspoons
Curry powder 1 teaspoon (optional)

Grind all vegetables and fruit in meat grinder using medium blade. Place in deep nonaluminum kettle and add remaining ingredients. Simmer until thick (approximately 1 hour). Skim and pack in hot, sterile jars, leaving 1 inch at top. Cap with hot, sterile lids. If any jars fail to seal, process in boiling water bath for 20 minutes after water returns to boiling, or in pressure cooker for 20 minutes at 10 pounds pressure. Makes 8 cups.

Nutritional value: 2 tablespoons contain 20 Calories. *This should not be used by diabetics or hypoglycemics.* If salt substitute and diet-pack tomatoes are used, 2 tablespoons contain 2 milligrams sodium.

Nutritional Information
(Appendix)

Table 6
Nutritional Value of Canned Fruit

Fruit	Serving Size (Diabetic Fruit Exchange)	Water Pack	
		Carb.	Cal.
Applesauce	½ cup	C13	50
Apple Slices	½ cup	C13	50
Apricots	4 halves plus 2 T. juice	C9	38
Apricot/Apple Slices	½ cup (2 halves apricots)	C11	44
Cherries	8 cherries plus ¼ cup juice	C9½	38
Berries:			
Blackberries	½ cup	C11	48
Boysenberries	½ cup	C11	48
Red Raspberries	½ cup	C10½	43
Strawberries	¾ cup	C10	40
Berry-Applesauce	½ cup	C12	49
Fruit Cocktail (Mixed Fruits)	½ cup	C12	48
Nectarines	½ plus 1 T. juice	C12	48
Peach Halves	2 plus 2 T. juice	C10	42

Light Syrup		Medium Syrup*		Sodium Content**
Carb.	Cal.	Carb.	Cal.	Mg.
C14½	56	C16	62	2
C14½	56	C16	62	2
C10½	44	C12	50	1
C12½	50	C14	56	2
C11	44	C12½	50	1
C12½	54	C14	60	1
C12½	54	C14	60	1
C12	49	C13½	55	1
C11½	46	C13	52	1
C13½	55	C15	61	1
C13½	54	C15	60	1
C13½	54	C15	60	4
C11½	48	C13	54	2

Continued on next 2 pages

Fruit	Serving Size (Diabetic Fruit Exchange)	Water Pack	
		Carb.	Cal.
Peach Slices	½ cup with juice	C10	42
Pear Halves 2½"	2 plus 2 T. juice	C12½	50
Pear Slices	½ cup	C12½	50
Pineapple Chunks	⅓ cup with juice	C11	45
Pineapple Slices	1 slice plus 1 T. juice	C10	43
Purple (Prune) Plums	2 plums with 2 T. juice	C11	45

* Must reduce portion for diabetics to ⅔ amount shown = 1 Fruit Exchange.
** Sodium content is similar with either syrup since sodium content of fruit juice is so low.

Source: Catherine Adams. *Nutritive Value of American Foods, in Common Units,* U.S. Department of Agriculture, Agricultural Handbook No. 456. U.S. Government Printing Office, 1975.

Light Syrup		Medium Syrup*		Sodium Content**
Carb.	Cal.	Carb.	Cal.	Mg.
C11½	48	C13	54	2
C14	56	C15½	62	1
C14	56	C15½	62	1
C12	49	C14	57	1
C11	47	C13	55	1
C12½	51	C14	57	1

Table 7
Nutritional Value of Fruit Packed in Fruit Juice

Fruit	Amount*	Un-sweetened		Medium Syrup		Pure Juice	
		Carb.	Cal.	Carb.	Cal.	Carb.	Cal.
Apple slices	½ cup	C8	32	C9	36	C10	40
Apricots	½ cup	C10	40	C11	44	C12 (Apple juice)	48
Grapefruit sections	½ cup	C9	36	C10	40	C10½ (Grapefruit juice)	42
Melons							
Cantaloupe	½ cup	C6½	28	C7½	32	C8 (Orange juice)	34
Watermelon	½ cup	C5	21	C6	25	C7 (Apple juice)	29
Nectarines	½ cup	C12	48	C13	52	C13½ (Orange juice)	54
Orange sections	½ cup	C11	44	C12	48	C12½ (Orange juice)	50
Peach slices	½ cup	C8½	36	C9½	40	C10½ (Apple juice)	44
Pear quarters	½ cup	C12½	50	C13½	54	C15 (Apple-Pear juice)	60

* 1 ounce juice allowed per ½ cup fruit

Table 8
Nutritional Value of Frozen Fruits

Fruit	Amount	Liquid Used	Grams Carbohydrate*	Calories*	Sodium mg.
Apple slices	½ cup	Medium syrup	16	62	2
Applesauce	½ cup	(recipe given)	16	62	2
Apricots	½ cup	Medium syrup	12	50	10
Cherries	½ cup	Medium syrup	12.5	50	1
Grapefruit sections	½ cup	Grapefruit juice	14.5	58	2
Nectarines	½ cup	Orange juice	15.5	62	4
Orange sections	½ cup	Orange juice	14.5	58	1
Peach slices	½ cup	Medium syrup	13	54	1
Pear slices/ quarters	½ cup	Medium syrup	15.5	62	2
Plums	½ cup	Medium syrup	14	57	1
Mixed fruits	½ cup	Medium syrup	15	60	6

* This assumes liquid is eaten along with fruit.

Table 9
Nutritional Value of Low Methoxy
Pectin Jams and Jellies

	Carbohydrate per Tablespoon	Calories per Tablespoon	Amount for Diabetic Exchange
Jams			
Apricot-Pineapple	3 grams	12	3½ Tablespoons
Orange-Blueberry	1.5 grams	6	7 Tablespoons
Pineapple	2 grams	8	5 Tablespoons
Strawberry	1.5 grams	6	6½ Tablespoons
Jellies			
Apple	3 grams	12	3½ Tablespoons
Grape	4 grams	16	2½ Tablespoons
Mint	2 grams	8	5 Tablespoons
Orange Juice	3 grams	12	3½ Tablespoons

Table 10
Nutritional Value of Regular
Pectin Jams and Preserves

	Carbohydrate per Tablespoon	Calories per Tablespoon	Amount for Diabetic Exchange
Jams			
Apple-Berry Jam	1.5 grams	6	6 Tablespoons
Apricot-Lemon Jam	2.5 grams	10	4 Tablespoons
Apricot Marmalade	3.5 grams	14	3 Tablespoons
Carrot Jam	2.5 grams	10	4 Tablespoons
Mixed Soft Fruit Jam	2.0 grams	8	5 Tablespoons
Plum Jam	2.0 grams	8	5 Tablespoons
Strawberry Jam	1.5 grams	6	6 Tablespoons
Preserves			
Apple Butter	4.0 grams	16	2½ Tablespoons
Cherry Conserve	4.0 grams	21	2½ Tablespoons
Dried Apricot and Peach-Apricot Preserves	7.0 grams	28	1½ Tablespoons
Dried Peach Preserves	5.5 grams	27	5 Tablespoons
Lemony Prune Butter	6.0 grams	24	1½ Tablespoons
Peach Butter	2.5 grams	10	4 Tablespoons
Raisin Apple Spread	5.0 grams	20	2 Tablespoons
Strawberry Date Nut Preserves	4.5 grams	27	2 Tablespoons

Table 11
Nutritional Value of
Honey-Syrup, Canned Fruits*

Fruit	Serving Size
Applesauce	½ cup
Apple slices	½ cup
Apricots	4 halves plus 2 Tablespoons juice
Apricot-Apple slices	½ cup
Cherries	8 cherries plus ¼ cup juice
Berries:	
Blackberries	½ cup
Boysenberries	½ cup
Raspberries, red	½ cup
Strawberries	¾ cup
Berry-Applesauce	½ cup
Nectarines	½ cup plus 1 Tablespoon juice
Peach halves	2 halves plus 2 Tablespoons juice

Honey Light Syrup		Honey Medium Syrup		Sodium
Carb.	Cal.	Carb.	Cal.	Mg.
C18½	72	C19½	76	2
C18½	72	C19½	76	2
C14½	60	C15½	64	1
C16½	66	C17½	70	2
C15	60	C16	64	1
C16½	70	C17½	74	1
C16½	70	C17½	74	1
C16	65	C17	69	1
C15½	66	C16½	70	1
C17½	71	C18½	75	1
C17½	70	C18½	74	4
C15½	64	C16½	68	2

Continued on next 2 pages

Fruit	Serving Size
Peach slices	½ cup with juice
Pear halves	2 halves plus 2 Tablespoons juice
Pear slices	½ cup
Pineapple chunks	⅓ cup with juice
Pineapple slices	1 slice plus 1 Tablespoon juice
Purple (Prune) Plums	2 plums plus 2 Tablespoons juice
Fruit Cocktail (Mixed fruits)	½ cup

* Not for use by diabetics or hypoglycemics.

Honey Light Syrup		Honey Medium Syrup		Sodium
Carb.	Cal.	Carb.	Cal.	mg.
C15½	64	C16½	68	2
C18	72	C19	76	1
C18	72	C19	76	1
C16½	67	C17½	71	1
C15½	65	C16½	69	1
C16½	67	C17½	71	1
C17½	70	C18½	74	1

U.S. and Metric Measurements

Approximate conversion formulas are given below for commonly used U.S. and metric kitchen measurements.

Teaspoons	x	5	= milliliters
Tablespoons	x	15	= milliliters
Fluid ounces	x	30	= milliliters
Fluid ounces	x	0.03	= liters
Cups	x	240	= milliliters
Cups	x	0.24	= liters
Pints	x	0.47	= liters
Dry pints	x	0.55	= liters
Quarts	x	0.95	= liters
Dry quarts	x	1.1	= liters
Gallons	x	3.8	= liters
Ounces	x	28	= grams
Ounces	x	0.028	= kilograms
Pounds	x	454	= grams
Pounds	x	0.45	= kilograms
Milliliters	x	0.2	= teaspoons
Milliliters	x	0.07	= tablespoons
Milliliters	x	0.034	= fluid ounces
Milliliters	x	0.004	= cups
Liters	x	34	= fluid ounces
Liters	x	4.2	= cups
Liters	x	2.1	= pints
Liters	x	1.82	= dry pints
Liters	x	1.06	= quarts
Liters	x	0.91	= dry quarts
Liters	x	0.26	= gallons
Grams	x	0.035	= ounces
Grams	x	0.002	= pounds
Kilograms	x	35	= ounces
Kilograms	x	2.2	= pounds

Temperature Equivalents

Fahrenheit	− 32	x 5	÷ 9	= Celsius
Celsius	x 9	÷ 5	+ 32	= Fahrenheit

U.S. Equivalents

1 teaspoon	= ⅓ tablespoon
1 tablespoon	= 3 teaspoons
2 tablespoons	= 1 fluid ounce
4 tablespoons	= ¼ cup or 2 ounces
5⅓ tablespoons	= ⅓ cup or 2⅔ ounces
8 tablespoons	= ½ cup or 4 ounces
16 tablespoons	= 1 cup or 8 ounces
⅜ cup	= ¼ cup plus 2 tablespoons
⅝ cup	= ½ cup plus 2 tablespoons
⅞ cup	= ¾ cup plus 2 tablespoons
1 cup	= ½ pint or 8 fluid ounces
2 cups	= 1 pint or 16 fluid ounces
1 liquid quart	= 2 pints or 4 cups
1 liquid gallon	= 4 quarts

Metric Equivalents

1 milliliter	= 0.001 liter
1 liter	= 1000 milliliters
1 milligram	= 0.001 gram
1 gram	= 1000 milligrams
1 kilogram	= 1000 grams

Bibliography

Adams, Catherine. *Nutritive Value of American Foods, in Common Units.* U.S. Department of Agriculture, Agricultural Handbook No. 456. Washington, D.C.: U.S. Government Printing Office, 1975.

Berto, Hazel. *Cooking with Honey.* New York: Crown Publishing Co., 1972.

Borella, Anne. *The How-To Book, Canning, Freezing and Drying.* Rev. Ed. New York: The Benjamin Co., Inc., 1976.

Dawson, Elsie H.; Gilpin, Gladys L.; and Fulton, Lois H. *Average Weight of a Measured Cup of Various Foods.* U.S. Department of Agriculture, Agricultural Research Service ARS 61-6. Washington, D.C.: U.S. Government Printing Office, 1969.

Fulwiler, Kyle D. *The Apple Cookbook.* Seattle: Pacific Search Press, 1980.

Gibbons, Euell, and Gibbons, Joe. *Feast on a Diabetic Diet.* Rev. Ed. Greenwich, Connecticut: Fawcett Publications, Inc., 1974.

Griswold, Ruth M. *The Experimental Study of Foods.* Boston: Houghton Mifflin Co., 1962.

Lesem, Jeanne. *The Pleasures of Preserving and Pickling.* New York: Knopf Publishing Co., 1975.

Lowe, Belle. *Experimental Cookery.* 4th Ed. New York: John Wiley & Sons, Inc., 1961.

MacRae, Norma M. *How to Have Your Cake—and Eat It, Too!* Rev. Ed. Anchorage: Alaska Northwest Publishing Co., 1982.

Pennington, Jean A.T., and Church, Helen N. *Bowes & Church's Food Values of Portions Commonly Used.* 13th Ed. New York: Harper & Row, 1980.

Walnut Acres Bulletin: "Low Sugar Jams and Jellies." Walnut Acres, Penns Creek, Pennsylvania. (Product information sheet)

General Index

(Recipe index follows on page 162)

sugar content of, 56

Paraffin, 124
Pectin
    and acid combination, 49, 50, 51
    calcium solution used with, 49, 52, 53, 54
    content of in fruits, 49, 50, 51, 53
    how to check for, 49, 51
    special low methoxy, 49, 51, 52, 53, 58
    sugar in, commercial, 52
Pickling
    choosing vegetables for, 21–25
    equipment needed for, 25, 26
    general information, 25–27, 88
Pineapple juice
    as sweetener for other fruits, 8, 9, 32–33
    sugar content of, 56
Pressure gauge, 25–26

Salt and salt substitutes, 11
Seal, how to check, 41
Sterilize, how to, 26–27
Storing home-canned fruit, 41–42
Sugar
    in commercial jams, 48

in commercial pectin, 52
in fruit juices, 56
preventing discoloration, 37, 42
removing from recipes, 48–49
sweetness of
    compared to honey, 13, 122
    compared to fruit juices, 13, 33
Syrup
    berry–syrup combinations, 36–37
    choosing and making, for canning, 31–33
        artificially sweetened, 32
        fruit-juice sweetened, 8, 13, 32
        no added sweetener, 32
    directions for making, with natural juice, 32–33
    for freezing fruits, 42–43
    honey, 9, 122–23

Vegetables
    choosing, for canning and pickling, 21–25
    choosing and preparing, for freezing, 46–48
Vinegar, 11, 51

Zucchini, for coloring other foods, 11

Recipe Index

Apple juice, as main ingredient in
    Apple Butter, 71
    Apple Jelly, 67
    Frozen Apple Jelly, 83
    Fruit Juice Sauce, 85
Apples
    choosing, for canning, 13–14, 16–17
    choosing and preparing, for freezing, 44
    home-canned, raw or cold pack, 34, 36
    recipes using
        Apple Butter, 71
        Applesauce, 34
        Applesauce with Honey, 123
        Basic Sugarless Vegetarian Mincemeat, 86
        Berry–Applesauce, 37
        Green Tomato Mincemeat, 87
        Meatless Mincemeat with Honey, 133
        Raisin–Apple Spread, 108
        Spiced Apples, 114
        Tangy Fruit Relish, 115
Applesauce, home-canned, hot pack, 34
    How to freeze, 44
    recipes
        Applesauce, 34
        Applesauce with Honey, 123
        Berry–Applesauce, 37
Apricots
    choosing, for canning, 14
    choosing and preparing, for freezing, 42, 43, 44

home-canned, raw or cold pack, 36
recipes using
    Apricot–Lemon Jam, 60
    Apricot Marmalade, 61
    Apricot–Orange Butter with Honey, 130–31
    Apricot–Pineapple Jam with Honey, 140
    Apricot–Pineapple Jam, 64
    Dried Apricot–Pineapple Preserves, 105
    Extra Good Apricot Butter, 106–7
    Jam-Pot Jam, 100
    Mixed Soft Fruit Jam, 62
    Tangy Fruit Relish, 115
Asparagus
    choosing, for canning and pickling, 21
    choosing and preparing, for freezing, 47

Beans
    choosing, for canning and pickling, 21
    choosing and preparing, for freezing, 47
    recipes using
        Mustard Pickles, 90
        Pickled Green Beans, 113
Beets
    choosing, for canning and pickling, 21
    recipes using
        Delicious Pickled Vegetable Salad, 110
        Mother's Beet–Cabbage Relish, 111

Other Cookbooks from Pacific Search Press

The Apple Cookbook by Kyle D. Fulwiler
Asparagus: The Sparrowgrass Cookbook by Autumn Stanley
The Bean Cookbook: Dry Legume Cookery by Norma S. Upson
The Berry Cookbook by Kyle D. Fulwiler
Bone Appêtit! Natural Foods for Pets by Frances Sheridan Goulart
The Carrot Cookbook by Ann Saling
The Crawfish Cookbook by Norma S. Upson
The Dogfish Cookbook by Russ Mohney
The Eggplant Cookbook by Norma S. Upson
A Fish Feast by Charlotte Wright
Food 101: A Student Guide to Quick and Easy Cooking by Cathy Smith
The Green Tomato Cookbook by Paula Simmons
Mushrooms 'n Bean Sprouts: A First Step for Would-be Vegetarians
    by Norma M. MacRae, R.D.
My Secret Cookbook by Paula Simmons
The Natural Fast Food Cookbook by Gail L. Worstman
The Natural Fruit Cookbook by Gail L. Worstman
One Potato, Two Potato: A Cookbook by Constance Bollen and
    and Marlene Blessing
Rhubarb Renaissance: A Cookbook by Ann Saling
Roots & Tubers: A Vegetable Cookbook by Kyle D. Fulwiler
The Salmon Cookbook by Jerry Dennon
Starchild & Holahan's Seafood Cookbook by Adam Starchild and James
    Holahan
Warm & Tasty: The Wood Heat Stove Cookbook by Margaret Byrd Adams
The Whole Grain Bake Book by Gail L. Worstman
Wild Mushroom Recipes by Puget Sound Mycological Society
The Zucchini Cookbook (3d Ed. Revised & Enlarged) by Paula Simmons